The Art of Framing

The Art of Framing

Managing the Language of Leadership

Gail T. Fairhurst

Robert A. Sarr

Jossey-Bass Publishers • San Francisco

Substantial discounts on bulk quantities of Jossey-Bass books are available to corporations, professional associations, and other organizations. For details and discount information, contact the special sales department at Jossey-Bass Inc., Publishers (415) 433–1740; Fax (800) 605–2665.

For sales outside the United States, please contact your local Simon & Schuster International Office.

 Manufactured in the United States of America on Lyons Falls Pathfinder Tradebook. This paper is acid-free and 100 percent totally chlorine-free.

Library of Congress Cataloging-in-Publication Data

Fairhurst, Gail Theus, date.
    The art of framing : managing the language of leadership / Gail T. Fairhurst, Robert A. Sarr. — 1st ed.
      p. cm.
    Includes bibliographical references and index.
    ISBN 0-7879-0181-4
    1. Leadership. 2. Communication in management.   3. Interpersonal communication. I. Sarr, Robert A., date. II. Title.
HD57.7.F353 1996
658.4'092—dc20   95–37020

Credits are on pp. 215–216.

FIRST EDITION
HB Printing 10 9 8 7 6 5 4 3 2 1

The Jossey-Bass
Business & Management Series

Contents

Preface

Leadership is a language game. So said management scholars Louis Pondy and Jeffrey Pfeffer in the seventies when they asserted that leadership's true impact is on human sentiment and understanding rather than on the bottom line. Leaders operate in uncertain, sometimes chaotic environments that are partly of their own creation: while leaders do not control events, they do influence how events are seen and understood. They are movers and shakers of their organizations, and their most important tools are symbolic and linguistic.

Leadership is a language game, one that many do not know they are playing. Even though most leaders spend nearly 70 percent of their time communicating, they pay relatively little attention to how they use language as a tool of influence. Technically grounded managers may talk a good game on technical matters. Trained in the knowledge and versed in the jargon of a particular field, they easily produce words and sentences that others seem to understand. But the ease with which they speak causes listeners to miss the fact that language cloaks, sedates, even seduces people into believing that many of the so-called facts of our world are objectively rather than socially created. No other reason can explain why the same market fluctuations are seen as problems for some and opportunities for others. No other reason can explain why new visions and programs become future realities in some companies and remain as pipe dreams in others. No other reason can explain why the same uttered words are treated as gospel coming from one leader but hot air coming from another.

The Art of Framing treats leaders as managers of the meanings for their world. In this book, we introduce the skill of *framing:* a quality of communication that causes others to accept one meaning over another. It is a skill with profound consequences for behavior that influences how we and others respond to the world in which we live. It is a skill that great leaders possess and one that most readers will readily recognize, yet it is a skill that is not often taught. Many believe that you either have framing skills or you don't. Not so. You can learn to manage meaning through framing; this book can teach you how.

Psychologists, pastors, advertisers, and politicians make their living framing the realities they want their clients and constituents to accept. These professionals recognize the power of framing to influence how others see and interpret reality. Those of us who lead and participate in organizations should also recognize the power of this skill. This book provides a wealth of information that will give leaders new freedom—and new responsibility—in everyday communication, both inside and outside the organization.

Our Research into Framing

Our research into the subject of framing first began in 1987 when Gail Fairhurst took up residence in the organization for which Bob Sarr worked. The organization was an inviting place to spend a university sabbatical because it had a reputation for hiring the best and brightest and was a consistent blue-chip performer in the consumer products field nationally and internationally. Known for its leading-edge work in the field of organizational development, it was one of the first to institute self-managing team-based systems, to wrestle with issues of empowerment and diversity, and to adopt the Total Quality Management (TQM) philosophy of W. Edwards Deming. The company was in the midst of TQM adoption at the time of our study. What better place to study how communication contributes to a high-performance organization?

We talked with countless leaders and their direct reports throughout the manufacturing arm of this organization and asked them to complete questionnaires. We tape-recorded many of their actual work conversations; our analyses of these conversations form one part of the research base of this book. Many of the conversations are valuable teaching tools, which is why we have chosen to include them. Those who spoke on tape expressed their views freely, probably because the conversations were tape-recorded in their own work settings without our presence and were not structured in any way.

Willing participants were simply told just to turn on the recorder the next time they expected a conversation to last more than a few minutes. In two separate data gatherings, we collected over two hundred conversations of approximately thirty minutes in length.

In spite of the sophistication of the company and the high level of professional training of its managers, the vast majority of the conversations were hit-or-miss when it came to constructing the right context or frames for management initiatives. Lost opportunities were frequent and apparent. It was in this astonishing discovery that we came to appreciate how leadership is realized in the everyday and routine aspects of the job—in a succession of moments rather than in landmark decisions. Leaders repeatedly appeared oblivious to golden opportunities to help others make sense out of events, to explain the why and wherefore of company decisions, and to secure commitment and buy-in from employees. Repeatedly, they missed opportunities to frame or reframe the negative framing practiced so skillfully by those who resist change.

Since our initial research in 1987, we have observed and spoken about framing communications and interviewed leaders and other professionals in a variety of organizations both in the United States and Europe. From these observations and conversations, we are convinced that our initial experience was not unique. Leaders everywhere can be numbed by the pressures and routines of their jobs. Or, because of their appreciation for framing everyday work issues, they can understand the power that lies within those routines. We are convinced that conversations like the ones we recorded and like those we have heard so many times are taking place in just about any company you could name.

Our research also included an intensive survey of the management and communication literature, focusing heavily on case studies, for examples of great and not-so-great framing by leaders. These case studies provided us with some framing examples that were highly creative. Finally, we looked beyond the management environment and the business pages and sought great examples of framing from the worlds of politics, sports, literature, entertainment, and religion. These too provided us with useful insights.

We think that after reading *The Art of Framing*, you will start to do your own research on framing because, like us, you will notice framing in every aspect of your life.

Who Should Read This Book?

The Art of Framing is written for all those who lead or aspire to lead in organizations today. Even if you are not currently a designated leader or manager, you can demonstrate leadership through mastering the framing skills in this book. If you aspire to leadership roles with greater responsibility, you will find this book useful. We believe that people become leaders through the ability to manage meaning. Indeed, all truly great leaders have mastered the skill of framing.

For all of you who seek to lead, the aim of our book is three-fold. First, we want you to understand how you shape your own realities and co-construct meaning through your everyday conversations with others. Second, if communication is the central function of leadership, there should be a message to communicate. Our goal is to help you be thoughtful about the messages you do send via your actions and words. Third, in light of the fact that you cannot carefully plan and script much of your daily communication, we will show you what you can do to become a more effective spontaneous communicator.

Overview of the Contents

Chapter One defines framing and establishes its importance. In this chapter, we introduce the three chief components of framing: language, thought, and forethought. We also distinguish framing from manipulation, with which it is sometimes inappropriately confused.

Chapter Two explores the principle that good framing starts from within. Our mental models form a foundation for all good framing. In this chapter, we show the consequences of working with underdeveloped mental models and the important role mental models play in formulating communication goals.

Chapter Three explores the mental models of particular importance to organizational leaders. It covers the development of mental models in support of an organizational vision and helps you deal with the daily demands for framing that vision. We will show you some techniques for the continuous development of your mental models and help you understand two different forms of reasoning that you will use in framing your vision for others.

Chapter Four shows how framing effectively and developing sensitivity to context go hand in hand. We offer six guidelines that will increase your sensitivity to context and your ability to identify good framing opportunities.

Chapter Five introduces a set of language tools—metaphors, jargon, catchphrases, contrast, spin, and stories—that will help you hone your framing skills. The assets and liabilities of each tool are explored. The chapter also enables you to sharpen your skills with these tools while focusing on the framing of your vision.

Chapter Six brings a cautionary note. All of us can and do mix our language tools, and sometimes this is done with powerful effect. However, when using tools in combination, we can create mixed messages. We can also create mixed messages when our language seems to contradict our behavior or when the expectations of others are not met by what we say or do. This chapter shows you how to avoid mixed messages of all varieties.

What percentage of your daily conversations do you consciously plan ahead of time? If you are like most people, the percentage is very small. Chapter Seven is about priming for spontaneity—preparing yourself mentally so that when opportunities present themselves, communication flows spontaneously. This chapter covers those situations that can be planned and those that are complete surprises.

In framing, credibility is crucial. In Chapter Eight, we will show you how credibility is established—and how it is destroyed—through what you frame, how you frame, and how others frame you. Then, in the Epilogue, we stress that framing opportunities occur often and that, with forethought, we can make the most of them. With reflection and continued effort, we can even reclaim those opportunities that escaped us or that sailed by unnoticed the first time.

Acknowledgments

Many individuals helped us along the way, and to all we are most grateful. We would, however, like to single out a few people. Peg Allensworth, Cathy Burns, Eric Eisenberg, Karen Horrell, Marilyn Kiracofe, Don Miller, Debbie Rumpke, and Susan Smyth read early versions of the manuscript; their comments were invaluable. Jack

Hoopes, Chuck Hundertmark, and Jerry Jordan supplied us with some excellent examples and insights. Thom Joyce, Barbara Reckers, Nuha Nasrallah, and Elisa Helm assisted us with preparing the manuscript even when it was inconvenient to do so. Thanks also go to Don Miller and Kathleen Reardon for their moral support. To Sarah Polster, our editor at Jossey-Bass, we are most grateful for her belief in this book from the beginning. Developmental editor Jan Hunter brought a level of excellence to the manuscript for which we are most appreciative. Her wisdom and wit made the writing and editing process more pleasurable and productive.

Finally, we are grateful to all of the family, friends, clients, and associates who, during the course of this project, received less than the full measure of our attention that each of them deserves. Without their patience and support, *The Art of Framing* would not have been possible.

November 1995

GAIL T. FAIRHURST
Cincinnati, Ohio

ROBERT A. SARR
Santa Fe, New Mexico

The Authors

Gail T. Fairhurst is professor of communication at the University of Cincinnati where, since 1992, she has also been head of the Department of Communication. She received her B.A. degree (1973) from Bowling Green State University in English, her M.A. degree (1975) from Ohio State University in communication, and her Ph.D. degree (1978) from the University of Oregon in communication. She has been on the faculty of the University of Cincinnati since 1979 and is a founding member of the Center for Environmental Communication Studies, located in the Department of Communication.

Fairhurst's scholarly work in both the communication and organizational sciences has been widely published. In 1994, she received a Speech Communication Association award for the best article in organizational communication, and she is a four-time recipient of recognition for a top paper in organizational communication at the International Communication Association Annual Conference. She has published in *Academy of Management Journal, Academy of Management Review, Organizational Science, Human Communication Research*, and *Communication Monographs*. Fairhurst is also author of numerous book chapters, including two chapters on the subjects of leadership and language in the forthcoming *New Handbook of Organizational Communication*. She has served on the editorial boards of *Human Communication Research, Communication Monographs, The Journal of Communication, Management Communication Quarterly*, and *Communication Quarterly*.

Fairhurst has consulted with numerous organizations including General Electric, the Kroger Company, Cincinnati Bell, and Children's Hospital of Cincinnati. Her most recent consulting work centers on the communication of organizational vision and mission statements and leadership development. She can be reached at (513) 556-4451 or fairhrst@uc.edu on the Internet.

Robert A. Sarr is chair and general manager of Santa Fe Southern Railway, a small and new freight and passenger railroad in Santa Fe, New Mexico. He also continues his work as an organizational consultant specializing in the creation of high-performance systems. Sarr received his A.B. degree (1964) from Drew University in economics and his M.B.A. degree (1966) from Stanford University.

Sarr's corporate career includes a full range of human relations–industrial relations assignments, with a five-year tenure as senior manager of employee relations. In the role of internal consultant, he has concentrated on redirecting and restructuring manufacturing sites and staff functions across a consumer goods company; this position provided the research material that initially sparked the writing of this book.

Sarr has consulted for numerous organizations across the United States and Canada; his clients include Procter & Gamble, Colgate-Palmolive, the Witt Company, and Southwestern Ohio Regional Transit Authority (SORTA). He has also consulted in Japan, the Philippines, and most Western European countries. He recently concluded a major intervention in a seven-site manufacturing organization in Europe.

A peripheral interest in railroads and mass transit led Sarr to become involved in Santa Fe Southern, where he is now getting the consultant's just reward of having to practice what he preached. He may be reached at (505) 989-8600.

The Art of Framing

Chapter One

Framing
Seizing Leadership Moments in Everyday Conversations

This is a book about leadership and communicating, about learning to select words and phrases that really mean something to the people we wish to lead or influence. Effective leaders present the world with images that grab our attention and interest. They use language in ways that allow us to see leadership not only as big decisions but as a series of moments in which images build upon each other to help us construct a reality to which we must then respond.

Many such leadership moments are etched in our memories. We remember John F. Kennedy's 1961 inaugural address when he said, "Ask not what your country can do for you; ask what you can do for your country." We remember Martin Luther King's "I Have a Dream" speech in the midst of the civil rights movement. We remember the vision of the "democratization of the computer," coined and advocated by the two young entrepreneurs who founded Apple Computer, Steve Jobs and Steve Wozniak. And we remember the heralded theme of "drive out fear" of W. Edwards Deming and the Total Quality Management (TQM) movement.

These are the makings of headlines. Yet everyday leaders lead every day and in every possible situation. They seize leadership moments when coffee-room talk of problems leads to a discussion of the choices made available by the new company program. They seize moments to describe the next steps in achieving unit goals, forming an agenda. They ensure that the company's mission is deftly described in terms of the day-in and day-out duties of an employee—and then take a few moments to say, "Okay, here's how this applies to you right now." Or they piece together new and existing company programs by initiating conversations such as, "Well, here's how Total Quality and our performance-appraisal system go together for me."

All leaders—famous or not—know that the simple but powerful lesson behind seizing leadership moments is to manage meaning. Uncertainty and ambiguity rear their heads often, thanks in part to the fast pace of change. In order to act, all of us are compelled to affix meaning to the environments in which we find ourselves—at work and in the world. We must make sense of a situation before we can know how to respond. Yet many individuals prefer to look to others to define what is real, what is fair, and what should count now and in the future. They are reluctant to manage meaning for themselves or others because there is risk involved when the stakes are high.

Leadership is about taking the risk of managing meaning. We assume a leadership role, indeed we become leaders, through our ability to decipher and communicate meaning out of complex and confusing situations. Our communications actually do the work of leadership; our talk is the resource we use to get others to act (Gronn, 1983). Do our communications lead others to see only constraints and roadblocks or to see opportunity? Leadership is all about taking the risks necessary to positively affect the work lives of others and move an organization forward.

In discussing the effectiveness of leaders, management scholar Louis Pondy (1978) emphasized that leaders' effectiveness lies in their "ability to make activity meaningful" for others; leaders "give others a sense of understanding what they are doing." As Pondy said, "If in addition, the leader can put [the meaning of behavior] into words, then the meaning of what the group is doing becomes a social fact. . . . This dual capacity . . . to make sense of things and to put them into language meaningful to large numbers of people gives the person who has it enormous leverage" (pp. 94–95).

This leverage is part of what distinguishes true leaders. Abraham Zaleznik (1977) was among the first to draw a distinction between managers and leaders, noting that managers pay attention to how things get done, while leaders pay attention to what events and decisions mean. Warren Bennis and Burt Nanus (1985) took this a step further and argued that leaders concern themselves with the organization's basic purpose and general direction and with articulating these ideas to others.

In addition, as many organizations have shifted toward greater employee empowerment and democratization, their communication environments have become significantly more dynamic and characterized by mutual influence and real dialogue than they were as recently as fifteen years ago. These factors lead us to an inescapable conclusion: to be effective leaders today, we must understand how to function as managers of meaning.

The skill that is required to manage meaning is called *framing*. In this first chapter, our goal is to introduce this skill to you. We want to show you that you do not have to be naturally eloquent or especially talented with language to succeed at framing. Framing is a skill that can be taught—and that you can learn.

What Is Framing?

The essential tool of the manager of meaning is the ability to frame. To determine the meaning of a subject is to make sense of it, to judge its character and significance. To hold the frame of a subject is to choose one particular meaning (or set of meanings) over another. When we share our frames with others (the process of framing), we manage meaning because we assert that our interpretations should be taken as real over other possible interpretations.

To understand this better, consider how gifted photographers show us their view of the world through their photographs. They capture a viewpoint for others to understand and appreciate. They focus their cameras and frame their subjects so that by seeing their photographs, others can know what each photographer intended.

Consider Dorothea Lange, who photographed images from the Great Depression. She wanted to show the mood or plight of Americans affected by those hard times. Lange did not take pictures of empty factories, abandoned farms, or large throngs of unemployed people. Instead, she placed in her viewfinder the faces of the people of the Depression. Her message was clear because she framed the Depression in terms of the individuals who were suffering.

Ansel Adams's message was the grandeur of the "Big country—space for heart and imagination," as he once said (*Great Photographers,* 1971, p. 214). Adams did not dwell on a solitary flower or a plowed field; there were no side trips into "little things." On the contrary, he placed enormous vistas in his viewfinder and used his technical and artistic skills to let us appreciate each vista's size and greatness.

Lange and Adams are great photographers not because of their subjects but because of their skill at framing, at transmitting their point of view. Just like a photographer, when we select a frame for a subject, we choose which aspect or portion of the subject we will focus on and which we will exclude. When we choose to highlight some aspect of our subject over others, we make it more noticeable, more meaningful, and more memorable to others. Our framing adds color or accentuates the subject in unique ways. For this reason, frames determine whether people notice problems, how they understand and remember problems, and how they evaluate and act upon them (Entman, 1993).

Frames exert their power not only through what they highlight but also through what they leave out. In framing, when we create a bias towards one interpretation of our subject, we exclude other aspects, including those that may produce opposite or alternative interpretations. On promoting "the office family" as a way to frame a company, for example, self-styled office anthropologist David Graulich noted, "Your mom doesn't lay you off. She doesn't say, 'We've had 30 great years together, but it's time to let you go. We're downsizing the family.'" (Leibovich, 1995, p. D3). With a bit of humor, Graulich shows us that framing also has the power to distort.

Constructing Reality Through Framing

In the complex and chaotic environments in which most of us work, often there is considerable maneuverability with respect to "the facts." Certainly, it is difficult to alter the reality of some events, such as an equipment breakdown. But if there is any uncertainty or ambiguity about, for example, why the equipment broke down, what is real is often what we say is real. What is important is what we choose to say is important.

This was a painful lesson learned during a training session at the Kroger Company, one of the nation's largest food retailers. A consultant was asked to lead twenty-four superstore managers in three days of communication and team building. Everything went pretty much as expected until everyone returned from lunch on the last day. Six of the seminar participants found that their table, chairs, and diplomas certifying their participation were all missing. As they and the consultant looked around in astonishment, a spokesman for the eighteen remaining class members said that the group, which they had named the Judas group (after the disciple who betrayed Jesus Christ), had gotten its just reward. "We no longer consider you a part of this class," the spokesman said boldly.

What could have produced this turn of events? The morning exercise had been based on an often-used game known as the "Prisoner's Dilemma," an exercise in which groups must choose whether to compete or cooperate with one another. If the groups cooperate, there is a win-win outcome. However, the gain by each group is small, and the cumulative gain of the class is moderate. If most groups choose cooperation and one chooses to compete, there is a win-lose outcome. The groups who choose cooperation lose, while the competitive group wins big—very big—and there is no cumulative gain for the class.

On the surface, the game is about figuring out who the team is. If the groups decide that the team is the individual group, they focus on getting points only for themselves and ignore the cumulative class points. If the group decides that the team is the entire class of four groups, all of the focus is on the cumulative score and not the individual group scores.

On a deeper level, the game is about constructing reality and, through framing, leading others to action. The exercise begins with a set of directions that are intentionally ambiguous, read only once by the consultant, and provide no opportunity for questions. The intent is to simulate uncertain business conditions. Those individuals with an early take on the purpose of the exercise emerge as opinion leaders. Multiple interpretations are certainly possible, but the opinion leaders are usually sure that only one is correct.

Right from the start, the Judas group had an opinion leader who offered the following interpretation of the situation: "The exercise directions said to win as many points as possible. It didn't say anything else. It means that we have to assume responsibility for our own survival, because we can't always trust others to look out for our interests. Look at Group Two over there. Do you trust those guys?"

Meanwhile, the remaining three groups initially considered the same position and sensed some of the same distrust the Judas group felt. However, their opinion leaders felt that the cumulative class scores, which were consistently turning up zero points due to win-lose game behavior, could not be ignored. At several points in the exercise, they spoke to their groups and the class as a whole. Here is what one opinion leader said: "The directions said win as many points as possible, but while you [the Judas group] are winning individual points, the class has no cumulative points. If this exercise is about individual group competition, why are cumulative points a part of this exercise? Can't you see what's going on here? This is an exercise about working together and cooperating as a class. We are many parts but we are all one body, and it's called the Kroger Company."

That argument proved futile with respect to the Judas group. They racked up a considerable individual group score while the other groups fell deep into the negative column. The latter groups felt betrayed; hence their naming of the Judas group. Having framed the Judas group as a bunch of traitors, the only logical response was to symbolically separate them from the class through removal of their chairs, tables, and diplomas.

The example of this game reveals ways in which reality is socially constructed. Since cues from the environment are often ambiguous, we are too often forced into making up the game as we go along, creating the reality to which we must then respond (Weick, 1979). Those individuals who think they understand the game and offer enticing or convincing opinions as to what it all means are those to whom we look for leadership. Certainly that was true for the Judas group when their opinion leader announced that the directions mean "we have to assume responsibility for our own survival." It was also true for the rest of the groups, especially when one of their opinion leaders said, "We are many parts but we are all one body, and it's called the Kroger Company." Two different frames of the situation, two different socially constructed realities.

Components of Framing:
Language, Thought, and Forethought

There are three key components of framing. *Language* is the most apparent component of the skill. The *thought* component refers to the internal framing we must do before we can frame for others. Finally, *forethought* is the secret ingredient that prepares us for on-the-spot framing.

Language in Action

A plumber we know used his backhoe to look for a broken sewer line under a neighbor's lawn and was successful in his search. When asked by the lady of the house, "How can you stand that stifling smell?" his reply was, "Smells like bacon and eggs to a plumber, ma'am." The plumber's frame of the situation, focusing on his economic gain, probably helps him tolerate a smell that most of us find repugnant.

As this example demonstrates, it is easy to create alternative views of the world with a mere turn of a phrase. Highlight the negatives, and a problem looks overwhelming. Accentuate the positives, and a solution seems just around the corner. Choose an image ("stifling smell"), and you have highlighted one aspect of your subject; choose another ("bacon and eggs"), and a new aspect emerges.

Our language choices are critical to the management of meaning through framing. Framing creates understanding, in part, because of how language works naturally (Alexander, 1969). Let's look at the ways language works for us:

• *Language helps in focusing, especially on aspects of situations that are abstract and only vaguely sensed at first.* For example, you may describe the problems that you face with a group of employees as "increased apathy," "low morale," or "a growing lack of confidence in management to do the right thing." These terms help stabilize and secure what are, at first, vaguely held perceptions.

• *Language helps us to classify and put things in categories.* Through our use of language, we categorize. We might, for example, frame someone's performance as marginal as opposed to above average or good.

- *Because our memory works through associations, language helps us to remember and retrieve information.* If you have ever been ticketed for speeding in a school zone, when you next see a sign that says "20 miles per hour" in a school zone, you're likely to remember that it means "20 miles per hour or a large fine." Thus, our memory is triggered by language.

- *Through metaphoric language, we can understand one thing in terms of another's properties, and so cross-fertilize our impressions* (Alexander, 1969). Take a second look at our plumber's "bacon and eggs" metaphor for the fumes that his digging releases. The suggestion that we transfer the smell of bacon frying to something so completely opposite is testimony to the power of metaphor!

But language alone cannot help us to become successful framers, because framing is the union of word and thought. To frame, we must also have a message—one to which we have given careful thought.

Thought and Reflection

In order to frame for others, we must first frame for ourselves. To frame internally, we draw upon our mental models. In his book *The Fifth Discipline,* Peter Senge (1990, p. 174) defines mental models as "deeply held internal images of how the world works." These images, which can range from simple generalizations to complex theories, have a powerful impact on our framing behavior because they affect what we see and, in turn, what we guide others to see.

Consider the following conversation between Don, a team leader in the organization that we studied, and Sally, a member of his team. Don shares with Sally the behaviors he notices in the team. Review the conversation, and you will see that the particular behaviors Don notices reflect his image (mental model) of ideal team functioning.

(1) *Don:*   But people seem to operate as if they're very restricted, and that's not right. The way that plays out is people want a lot of strong, clear direction.

(2) *Sally:* Yeah.

(3) *Don:*   But I have a picture of the process I want this team-based organization to follow. And one of the things

that I am consciously choosing not to do is to give direction, because I want us to struggle a little bit. I know that it is a struggle for the organization. I've offered a couple suggestions about possible goals for the future, but I have not prescribed that yet. The way I tend to operate is, if we are in some kind of crisis mode, as was often the case in my last job, then I am prescriptive if necessary. I would say frequently, "Here's what we have to do."

(4) *Don:* My sense is that we're not in a crisis mode, so we have ample time and opportunity for involvement, participation, wrestling with the issues, and being a little frustrated with why we're not where we want to be. And my desire is that we, as a group, would say, "Hey, we are just not happy with where we are. We want to do something about that." And I'm waiting on our module to decide that.

(5) *Sally:* I see what you are saying.

(6) *Don:* This is very different for me. So one of the things that I keep telling myself is that this is a learning experience of being in a role that's not a crisis situation and giving the organization the space it needs.

(7) *Sally:* Mm-hmm.

(8) *Don:* I get frustrated when people come in and talk with me on this project or that project, whatever it is, people are really looking for me to give them an answer.

(9) *Sally:* The right answer [*laughs*].

(10) *Don:* The right answer [*laughs*]. Since I have a lot of history of doing that, I'm still trying to be patient, but it is hard work because a part of me likes being in the driver's seat.

(11) *Sally:* What you are doing is clearly different from previous leaders, previous managers. Actually, we haven't had many leaders. We have had managers, which would be the more directive-type person. And you are right; people have gotten used to that.

Don's mental model of desired team processes reflects a self-managing team philosophy and includes qualities such as "involvement," "participation," "wrestling with the issues," and "being . . .

frustrated" *(4)*. Don sees rigidity in his team's behavior because these qualities are absent; this, in turn, leads him to frame the team's behavior as "not right" *(1)*. Don also has a mental model for crisis situations that enabled him to determine that the group was "not in a crisis mode" *(4)*. Thus, we can see how Don's mental models influence what he sees and how he frames the situation for Sally.

Sally has mental models as well; hers lead her to frame leaders as different than managers. A mental model is an essential resource: it identifies the dimensions along which our experiences will be judged and subsequently communicated to others.

It is important to bring our mental models to the conscious level. Without that step, our mental models may be limiting; incorrect assumptions about the world may escape our notice. So, whenever possible, we must think through our mental models in advance of our need for them.

Forethought and Spontaneity

Although it is not emphasized in most communication training, the reality is that to be effective, leaders at any level must communicate spontaneously—anytime, anywhere. They must know how to handle a wide range of people and situations in split-second moments of opportunity, when there is no time for carefully scripted speeches—only time to break into the conversation and frame. In a recent interview, Herb Kelleher (Lee, 1994, p. 65), CEO of the highly successful Southwest Airlines, said it well: "There's a lot being said about the importance of communication. . . . But it can't be rigid; it can't be formal. It has to proceed directly from the heart. It has to be spontaneous, it has to be between individuals seeing each other on the elevator. 'Communication' is not getting up and giving formal speeches."

Here's the paradox: the time to exert control over our spontaneous framing is not when we're about to communicate, but when we are storing our memories. To explain this better, let's return to the conversation between Don and Sally, which we know was not planned ahead of time. Don was effective at communicating his mental models because he exerted control over his communications well before he spoke to Sally: he used a process called priming.

Just as you prime a pump before the water comes out, Don primed his unconscious mind before the words came out. As a result of his recent job change, Don had been forced to consider his mental models about how teams function in crisis and noncrisis situations. By becoming more conscious of his mental models, he primed them for use in spontaneous communication with Sally.

Priming produces the state of readiness that is critical for effective spontaneous communication. Don's new job brought his mental models to the surface so that he did not need conscious control of his automatic and spontaneous communication. You can do the same, without changing jobs—in later chapters, we will show you how.

Powerful Framing in Action

Once you become sensitized to the concept of framing, you will be surprised at how often you will notice instances of framing, whether effective or ineffective. After analyzing countless examples, we have drawn four conclusions about powerful framing in action:

1. Framing increases the chances of achieving goals.
2. Framing requires initiative.
3. Framing is for everybody.
4. Framing opportunities are everywhere.

From getting buy-in on a new concept to achieving specific goals, framing is a powerful tool, available to everyone, in any circumstance.

Increasing the Chances of Achieving Goals

The path to goal achievement through framing is built on the fact that when the right frames are in place, the right behavior will naturally follow. This was beautifully demonstrated several years ago when the crisis in the U.S. auto industry peaked. Chrysler executives needed to convince Congress to grant $2.7 billion in loan guarantees to Chrysler, a private corporation that was not an essential part of the national defense establishment. The task was daunting, for Congress was inherently fearful of direct financial support of a private business. In addition, if someone had delivered a pure recitation of numbers and trends, Congress would have been numbed.

How, then, was Congress moved to act? One critical factor was that Lee Iacocca reframed the congressional members' thinking and removed their barriers to his goal of a bailout. Iacocca's message, which was often laced with metaphoric language, was quite simple: help Chrysler out at a relatively low cost or prepare for the bankruptcy of the tenth-largest company in the United States and the subsequent loss of six hundred thousand jobs. Iacocca used hard numbers to convince Congress; as he put it, "we bottom-lined them" (Iacocca and Novak, 1984, p. 208). He cited a Treasury Department estimate of the cost of a Chrysler collapse: $2.7 billion in the first year alone in unemployment insurance and welfare payments. Moving away from framing the issues solely around numbers, he also said, "If it makes sense to have a safety net for individuals, it makes sense to have a safety net for their companies. . . . Work, after all, is what keeps individuals alive" (p. 208).

Think for a moment about these few brief statements. Why did Iacocca mention six hundred thousand jobs and frame Chrysler as the tenth-largest company in the United States? The answer is simple. By framing Chrysler in terms of its absolute and relative size, he underscored the magnitude of the problem. He developed this further when he "bottom-lined them" with dollar figures and the numbers of lost jobs. Thus, with the frames of size and bottom line, he created a need and rationale for action.

Why did he draw an analogy between having a safety net for individuals and a safety net for their companies? Through this framing, he put faces on a faceless corporation. He reminded his audience that companies comprise people and people need work in order to survive. Chrysler's survival was thus essential to many individuals' well-being, not just to the survival of a faceless monolith. In reality, Iacocca did a lot more than "bottom-line" Congress. In powerful ways, he highlighted both the economic and human sides of his subject and got everyone involved.

Iacocca continued to draw Congress and the country in when he suggested that Chrysler's plight was not unique, that other industries were also in trouble. He framed Chrysler's problems as "our problems, the country's problems." Chrysler was a "microcosm of what was going wrong in America." Its problems were merely "the tip of the iceberg" facing American industry. From this foundation, he then framed the Chrysler bailout as a "test lab for everybody else" (Iacocca and Novak, 1984, p. 200).

Iacocca's message was that the picture was grim yet hopeful and terribly important because we would all be affected. The technique Iacocca employed to communicate his message is called identification, which encourages others to identify with our cause and feel "we are all in this together." If successfully used, identification helps strike down barriers to action.

Iacocca helped to change the frames of Congress and of many Americans by combining rational and emotional appeals. He skillfully blended facts and numbers to underscore the size of the problem; he also used metaphors to create memorable images that tugged at American values. References to "America," "icebergs," "test labs," "safety nets," "microcosms," and the like made for appealing and easily comprehended images.

Iacocca's framing was sensible, memorable, and not easily refuted in the minds of Congress or the American public. He provided a definitive, affirmative answer to the question, "Should Chrysler be saved?" and so received the assistance he requested. His experience powerfully demonstrates the way framing assists us in goal achievement: when the right frames are in place, the right behavior naturally follows.

As we will later see, Iacocca's impact is not always regarded in such a positive light. But in the bailout, he did find a way to inspire others to help. This did not happen without effort: developing those frames and putting them in place required a powerful amount of initiative.

The Importance of Initiative

In a recent series of *Harvard Business Review* articles on the changing role of top management, management experts Christopher Bartlett and Sumantra Ghoshal (1994) wrote about a new breed of CEOs who reject a clinical framing of the company's objectives. Instead, these CEOs give people the freedom to interpret the company's objectives broadly and creatively. They encourage those in the organization to "interpret, refine, and make operational" the corporate ambition. One such CEO, Andy Grove of Intel, learned the benefit of this as lower-level managers effected the company's shift from memory chips to microprocessors some two years before upper management really caught on. On the need for more interpretive flexibility of company objectives, he said, "We need to soften the strategic focus at the top so we can generate new possibilities from within the organization" (Bartlett and Ghoshal, 1994, p. 82).

Grove is asking people to take the initiative in framing the company's objectives to take advantage of new entrepreneurial opportunities. Interestingly, some of this same initiative appears necessary in reengineering efforts in which management experts urge organizational change agents to "continuously formulate and reformulate a vision for both the near and far term that ensures the necessary linkages among the vision, mission, and operations" (Hitt, Keats, Harback, and Nixon, 1994, p. 19). All of this requires a vision that evolves through continuous framing of the organization's goals versus its current situation.

Whether one frames company objectives to seize entrepreneurial opportunities, continuously frames and reframes a vision to size the organization at the best levels, or frames for any of one hundred other reasons, framing is an activity that requires initiative for maximum impact. That initiative must have both purpose and perspective in appropriate measure.

Purpose comes from being clear about your goals for the situation at hand. It also comes from being clear about your role in the big picture of what the company is about and where it's headed. In many ways, big-picture framing was Iacocca's genius: he convincingly spelled out that the fate of the country and Chrysler were intertwined and that a common set of values was shared by all. While other managers suppress or ignore issues of mission, vision, and values because the problems at hand look too trivial or too daunting, effective leaders define these issues in the midst of problem solving and so contribute in a direct fashion to purposeful organizational behavior.

Effective framers know the perspective of their audience and take seriously the question, "For whom am I managing meaning?" This is not just asking, "What's the situation?" but, "What's their situation?" Again, Bartlett and Ghoshal's point about avoiding clinically framed company objectives applies. Slick but clinical packaging of the company's mission, vision, values, programs, or strategies may fall on deaf ears unless these ideas can be made personally meaningful and relevant to the individual. Effective framers make sure that the question, "How does this apply to me?" does not go unanswered.

In considering the perspective of others, we must ask at least the following questions:

- What are their mental models and are they aware of them?
- What situations and beliefs created their models?
- How firmly are those models held?

To truly consider the other's perspective requires us to have a high level of flexibility and to take the initiative. If anything about the company's mission, vision, values, programs, or strategies is at issue, we have to risk either its rejection or its evolution in attempting to address the other's needs.

In their book, *Leaders,* Warren Bennis and Burt Nanus wrote, "We believe that we human beings are suspended in webs of significance that we ourselves have spun" (1985, p. 112). This statement captures the socially constructed nature of reality, indicates the importance of initiative, and underscores that framing is for everybody.

Framing Is for Everybody

In Lee Iacocca, we have shown how one very visible CEO engaged in framing. But framing is used successfully by many others; in fact, the point we wish to stress is that all leaders at all levels must know how to frame. To frame properly, people must know how to communicate and how to interpret others' communications and frames.

Ruth, a young manager in manufacturing, is highly regarded, known as a "people person," and very committed to achieving production results. In the following conversation, Ruth communicates from her position—in the middle, between the demands of two corporate programs and the needs of Stephanie, one of her direct reports who is charged with program implementation.

Stephanie has just returned from a seminar on Deming's Total Quality Management and has several questions about conflicts she perceived between Deming's concept of TQM (particularly the fourteen points that make up Deming's philosophy) and High-Commitment Work Systems (HCWS), a program that introduced self-managing teams into the organization.

Though it is important to know what TQM and HCWS stand for in the context of this example, this conversation could be about any corporate program in use today. Here is a portion of the actual recorded conversation:

Stephanie: And some of this stuff went against High-Commitment Work Systems, which confuses me. Which one are we gonna do, you know? People say both. I say, "Wait a minute. Not according to Deming. You can't do both."

Ruth: Yeah, I think we can use his basic principles, but management isn't going to go in and change everything around. Do you know what I mean?

Stephanie: Deming says, "If you don't do these fourteen points to the letter, it's not going to work." And that confused me because what we're doing here is taking a piece of it.

Ruth: Yeah.

Stephanie: We're not going to cut our yearly performance appraisals, are we? I don't believe that.

Ruth: I think we'll cut out ranking, but that doesn't mean we'll cut out feedback.

Stephanie: A lot of this went against what we learned in basics [training for new managers]. It felt like when you start training as a new hire all over again, because everything I learned is wrong. So, I just need to know how serious we're going to get with these fourteen points.

Ruth: Well, we already have our own points. I mean we've changed Deming's points. You've seen that, haven't you?

Stephanie: I didn't see that.

Ruth: It's like we have nine points or something.

Stephanie: Teresa told me it's six, we took six and condensed the fourteen. See, Deming's saying, "Don't do that!" and we did it. That's weird to me.

Ruth: Mm-hmm.

Stephanie: I mean, we're doing what he says, and we're not doing
what he says. We're doing part of it, not all of it. And
he's saying, "Either all or nothing."

Ruth: Why don't we talk through what we need to do this
week before we get into expectations?

In this conversation, Ruth failed to appreciate the fact that
Stephanie's mental images for the two programs were contradictory for her. It is likely that Ruth was caught off guard and surprised by Stephanie's barrage of questions or was just too busy to
respond because of the demands of her production schedule. It is
also likely that Ruth was given neither the time nor the active support of management to develop her mental models for these two
programs and possibly to frame them as compatible. So, in conversation after conversation, missed opportunities to communicate
effectively about the programs accumulate daily and push them
toward failure, inch by inch.

The second reason why framing is for everybody concerns how
we interpret the framing that we receive from others. To lead effectively, we must also become astute judges of others' framing. Consider, for example, the role of the organizational consultants who,
like therapists and clergy, are in the business of reframing. Often
their goal is to promote organizational change, one example of
which is downsizing. Once a child of the recession and a tool to
reduce production workers, downsizing now occurs primarily to
eliminate unnecessary layers or non–value added positions
throughout an organization. As this shift in reasoning occurred,
the consultants' framing and terminology shifted from "downsizing" to "rightsizing" and "reengineering." The revised frames sub-
tly legitimized major reorganization efforts that were not recession
driven.

At Hallmark Cards, a group of consultants first had to frame
what was wrong in the organization in order to position the company for rightsizing. They produced a series of videotapes for Hallmark's forty top executives, the point of which was to show how
vulnerable the company was to losing market position (Stewart,
1993). One videotape began with small retailers describing declining store traffic. It then moved on to a senior vice president of
Wal-Mart, an important customer, raising some doubts about

whether the business relationship between Wal-Mart and Hallmark could continue. In their presentation, the consultants carefully managed the meaning of what was wrong in the organization. According to Steve Slanton, the CSC Index consultant who commissioned the videotapes, "By the time the lights went up, the temperature in the room had fallen 20 degrees" (Stewart, 1993, p. 44). Clearly, the Hallmark managers judged the consultants' framing to be credible and saw a need to change.

The management consultant is just one of many who seeks a measure of influence in today's organizations. To interact effectively with all those who frame for us, we must become astute at judging others' frames in order to appropriately sort out what is of value, what is irrelevant, and what may truly be harmful to our causes. We must also become alert to a multitude of framing opportunities.

Opportunities Are Everywhere

Think of the oft-repeated question, "Why is it that we don't have time to do anything right around here, but we always have time to do it over?" This question, frequently aimed at management, has great meaning for the subject of framing. When we find ourselves facing an issue that has arisen unexpectedly and for which we are unprepared, we often have to do things over again; instead, we should have done them right the first time.

As we saw in the conversation between Ruth and Stephanie, it is clear that Ruth mismanaged the opportunities that presented themselves there. Unfortunately, even if Ruth goes back to Stephanie just days later to correct the confusion, Stephanie will likely have had a chance to spread her doubts and concerns to others. It is also likely that she may have received reinforcement from those who are inclined to fault managerial initiatives of any kind. How much better would it have been had Ruth redirected the conversation and done some spontaneous framing of the issues?

The failure to see framing opportunities every time we communicate comes from equating talking with communicating. Many people believe that talking guarantees that we have connected with another. But talking guarantees little unless we take into account the perspective of the other and grasp the meanings that must be managed. Ruth wasn't conscious of managing meaning and so lost that opportunity; most of us do the same. We must be alert to opportunities to manage meanings that are relevant, personal, and appropriate so that they don't bypass people.

As we begin to appreciate our role as managers of meaning, we will act on our instincts to seize more framing opportunities. Over time, and with the techniques set out in later chapters, you will come to know when an issue is unnecessarily complex for others and will be able to seize a framing opportunity that simplifies it. You will know or suspect if there is misleading or suppressed information and can seize a framing opportunity to set the record straight. You will sense a broken connection and will seize a framing opportunity to forge linkages. Finally, you will know if barriers to action exist and will seize a framing opportunity to find a new angle that removes them. The meanings created through your framing with others will be tailored, personal, and full of impact—in short, they will be managed.

Leading Through Framing

Many individuals in organizations are seeking frames to put their world in order. In most matters, people are not rigidly defending old frames but are doing their best with current frames that are incomplete, a best guess, or otherwise inadequate. As we said earlier, when work environments do not make sense, everyone turns to the leaders within the organization for meaningful frames of events.

When our framing is full of meaning and influential, the opportunity to lead presents itself in several ways.

• We can create understanding, which is the basis for action. Through mutual understanding, collective behavior is made possible. People understand the similarities and differences in shared meanings but choose nonetheless to act in a concerted fashion.
• We can enable belief in one constructed frame to prevail over another. As the Judas group demonstrated in the example of one group framing another, reality is a social construct, and language is its primary vehicle. Without the framing of one group as

apart from the rest, the seminar's outcome would have been entirely different.

• We can perform many functions of leaders. We can, for instance, frame in order to explain, to gain attention and interest, to influence and inspire, and to promote identification with the organization.

Framing skills are fundamental to our ability to communicate. Just as we can tighten our writing skills, increase our vocabularies, polish our public speaking, or refine our interpersonal skills, we can develop and fine-tune our ability to frame. And we must, for framing is the resource we use to lead others to act. Framing is also key to how others view us and how effective we can be.

Watching Your Leadership

Make no mistake: others frame you based upon how you frame on a daily basis. If you frame without well-developed mental models and/or frame inconsistently, your work will be tagged as poorly thought out. If there are inconsistencies between how you frame and how you behave, your framing will be disregarded. Your behavior will be seen as the more powerful message. If you frame in order to manipulate, your intentions will be read.

Manipulation can be especially risky and destructive of both the perpetrators and their companies. It does seem reasonable, however, to ask whether the management of meaning through framing is just a form of manipulation. If I choose my words or my examples in order to change the way that you think, isn't this manipulation, pure and simple?

Being Alert to Manipulation

The question of framing as manipulation is not the dilemma it may first appear to be, for two key reasons. First, framing is not inherently good or bad until intention enters into the picture. The intention underlying framing differentiates manipulation in the pejorative sense of the word from the managing skill that is essential to communicating effectively. Does the plumber's comment, "smells like bacon and eggs to a plumber, ma'am," seem to be a manipulative reframing of a neighbor's comment about the "stifling smell"? Probably not, because there appears to be no intent on the part of the plumber to mislead or do harm.

Second, as this chapter has argued, there is a lot less certainty about what is factual than many would have us believe. Considering different frames on a subject is less about tampering with what is really real and more about acknowledging the plausibility of multiple realities or perspectives. Much as those in the Judas group quickly discovered, the way we look at things often determines reality. And one reality isn't necessarily more manipulative than another—just different.

Our values determine what and how we frame for others and, in turn, the kind of leader we are judged to be. Thus, we need to have our values firmly in mind as we develop our framing skills. If we have little of substance to say, a polished presentation means little. If we mask our intentions, a polished presentation destroys credibility and trust. And without trust, there is talking but little communication.

A Backward Glance at This Chapter

This chapter focused on the use of language and the role it plays in constructing reality through the management of meaning. In talking of seizing the initiative and communicating powerfully, it made the following points:

- Framing is a way to manage meaning. It involves the selection and highlighting of one or more aspects of our subject while excluding others.
- Since the function of leadership is the management of meaning, leaders must become experts at this skill.
- Of the three components of framing—language, thought, and forethought—the language component is the most tangible. It helps us to focus, classify, remember, and understand one thing in terms of another.
- The thought component of framing is essential to the development and use of our mental models. We must frame for ourselves before we frame for others.
- The forethought component of framing involves *priming* as an activity and prepares us to communicate spontaneously.

- Framing increases our chances of implementing goals and getting people's agreement, because once the right frames are in place, the right behavior follows.
- Framing requires initiative, which includes both a clarity of purpose and a thorough understanding of those for whom we are managing meaning.
- Framing is for everybody.
- Opportunities for framing occur with every communication.
- Our values play an important role in the kind of framing that we do and in the way that we (and our frames) are perceived.

As we have come to see, effective framing starts from within. To help you develop your framing skills, the next chapter takes up the subject of mental models and their importance to framing.

Chapter Two

From the Inside Out
How Your Own View of Reality
Shapes Communication Goals

Leaders who understand their world can explain their world. That is the principle that makes mental models important to communication. Mental models of how the world works (or is supposed to work) help us to size up situations and formulate our goals for communicating. This enables us to decide what and how we choose to frame.

Many people in organizations treat goal setting as a yearly activity in which they produce written statements about the results they intend to accomplish over the coming year. But this is not the only kind of goal setting. While we set goals for the tasks or results that we intend to achieve, we also set relationship and identity goals. And we can achieve most of these task, relationship, and identity goals through our communications.

This chapter focuses on the communication goals that are necessary to reach these three broader categories of goals. It also focuses on the important role of mental models in formulating our communication goals. As we will later learn, when we develop our mental models and become more aware of our communication goals, we increase our influence. Rather than deny ourselves the opportunity to be truly effective by relying on makeshift or flimsy models, we can strengthen our mental models. We can develop and use frames that are strong enough to support our communication goals.

Communication Goals and Our View of Reality

Mental models are deeply held internal images of how the world works. In any given situation, we determine what to say by applying those models (which are general) to the context (which is specific). Communication goals are a product of our general models and of the specifics of context, including its opportunities and constraints. We can represent that in very simple terms as

COMMUNICATION   =   MENTAL   X   SPECIFIC CONTEXT
    GOAL   MODELS   (OPPORTUNITIES &
                                      CONSTRAINTS)

When we decide on a communication goal, we are at a pivotal point between introspection and action. We will use our mental models to make sense of the context, but for what reason? We will go on to manage meaning, but why? Our communication goals lie at the crossroads between what we think and what we are about to say. Thus, in setting our communication goals, whether they revolve around tasks, relationships, or identities, we are making choices for the kind of impact we want to have.

Task Goals

In an organizational setting, the most familiar communication goals are those having to do with tasks. *Task goals* refer to the immediate opportunity or problem that defines the task of the situation. Conversations like the following one between a first-line supervisor, Jack, and a machine operator, Hal, reflect a typical task-related conversation. Jack's questions reflect a monitoring of Hal's performance as the work shift changes in their plant:

Jack: So, you're getting a pretty good crust now?
Hal: Yeah.
Jack: Do you think that the work on the fans—
Hal: The work on the fans isn't quite finished, but I think it helped a lot.
Jack: How about the spray water stuff?
Hal: Okay. We got that problem corrected temporarily. A new part has been ordered.

In order to get others to take action with respect to our tasks, we formulate communication goals much as Jack and Hal have done. Jack is concerned with eliciting and Hal is concerned with conveying the status of various responsibilities that Hal manages. In this case, the task goals occur in the context of paid employment, but they can occur in many other settings where work is being done.

Relationship Goals

A second type of goal is specifically concerned with establishing and maintaining relationships with others. For example, do you show equality, dominance, deference, closeness, distance, politeness, or brashness toward others with whom you work? Do you treat everyone in the same manner, regardless of his or her position?

Sometimes we communicate directly about our relationships, as when someone says after a disagreement, "I think we started off on the wrong foot. Can we try again?" This communication explicitly frames the relationship as beginning poorly. Most of the time, however, *relationship goals* are not expressed directly in what is said but indirectly in how something is said (Watzlawick, Beavin, and Jackson, 1967). Our tone of voice, facial expression, and gestures add information to our verbal communication about the relationship, even if the words deal only with the task. For example, try saying the words, "That's a thorough proposal," as a compliment. What do you notice about your nonverbal communication? Most of us would say that we looked directly at the other person, smiled, and had a rather pleasant tone of voice. Now say the same words and mean it as an insult. How has your nonverbal communication changed? You likely rolled your eyes and looked displeased. Note that it was not what you said that influenced whether it was a compliment or an insult; it was how you said it.

Here's another example. Joan is a department manager in a manufacturing plant where Rick is a team leader. They are talking about a new manager coming on board, someone to whom Rick will eventually report. In this dialogue, they are negotiating the role that Rick will assume until the new manager becomes fully operational. Notice how both refrain from stating an expectation or making a request of the other until each has addressed the other's previous point:

Speaker	Dialogue	Explanation
Rick	*Well, I understand what you are saying as far as the maintenance and getting his feet wet. But I think he needs to jump in with both feet and know what's going on in the project too.*	Rick expresses understanding, then states his expectation.
Joan	*Right. I mean he's got to be aware of what's going on there. But since you're handling a lot of that now, and as long as that's still okay, then allowing time to get his feet wet won't create an overload situation.*	Joan expresses agreement and understanding, then states her expectation.
Rick	*Well, I'm getting there myself* [laughter]. *It depends on how long it takes for him to be "qualified." Also, when do I start reporting to him? As far as I see it, I still should report to you until he is up to speed.*	Rick uses humor, then states his expectation.
Joan	*Agreed. But I want to make sure he gets enough time to get going, so that doesn't end up hurting us in the end.*	Joan expresses agreement, then states her expectation.
Rick	*Oh yeah.*	

Rick and Joan's statements of agreement, understanding, and humor are expressions of politeness. They are strategically positioned, out of concern for the working relationship, before requests or expectations are stated. It was well within Joan's power to dictate to Rick the terms of the new manager's role, and it is not inconceivable that Rick could have resisted strongly. Instead, both took pains to address the other's concerns and showed concern for the relationship in the process.

Identity Goals

A third type of goal is specifically concerned with identity. *Identity goals* refer to the self-image that we wish to present in our conversations. For example, do we present ourselves as competent, hard working, independent, fair minded, trustworthy, or amusing? In the same way that we communicate about our relationships in both direct and subtle ways, we do the same with our identities. For example, to frame ourselves as knowledgeable, we can be direct: "I know a lot about this subject." We can be subtle by building arguments with strong evidence and sound reasoning, which presents an inference of being knowledgeable. Or we can let slip bits of information that indirectly associate us with prestigious schools, advanced degrees, or people in high places.

Explicitly or implicitly framed, our identity is frequently an issue in conversation because we want others to support the implicit or explicit self-image that we project (Goffman, 1955). If I frame myself as knowledgeable, I lose face if someone challenges that self-image by showing my knowledge to be faulty or lacking. Causing another to lose face may be unavoidable at times, although strong cultural norms in America suggest that one goal of relationships is to help others save face.

Consider the following conversation between Ray, a warehouse supervisor, and Len, his direct report. They are discussing an incident in which Len chewed out a team member named Mitchell in front of the team. Notice how each manages his own and the other's identity in a specific way:

Speaker	Dialogue	Explanation
Ray	*Your jumping on Mitchell in front of the team like that was a little heavy handed, wouldn't you say?*	Ray frames Len's action as heavy handed.
Len	*Now it looks heavy handed, but with the information that I had at the time, it was justified.*	Len reframes it as justified.
Ray	*You hit the nail on the head, Len. You acted without having all the data in front of you.*	
Len	*Yes, but I can't tell you how many times Mitchell's had it coming.*	

Speaker	Dialogue	Explanation
Ray	*You can't excuse your mistake with Mitchell's past antics. What you did was human, but the lesson from this is to make sure you've got all of the data in front of you. I can understand if you feel a little defensive, but I'm just trying to help you understand how you can avoid future problems.*	Ray frames Len's action as human and Len's feelings as defensive.
		Ray frames himself as trying to help.

In this conversation, Ray and Len negotiate their identities unfailingly. Len counters Ray's "heavy handed" charge with "justified," while Ray, in turn, presents himself as "trying to help." Clearly, each cares about the image he presents.

Usually some image of ourselves is on the line when we interact with others. Sometimes we don't care about that image; other times, we care deeply.

Managing the Time Dimension of Goals

Our communication goals have a time dimension that is related to the scope of the goals that we set. Some of our goals are global or long term, others are short term, and still others are emergent (Wilson and Putnam, 1990). Task, relationship, and identity goals can fall in any of the time dimensions. For a closer look at the time dimension, let us examine global, short-term, and emergent task goals more closely.

Global Goals

Global goals are long term in nature and apply to a series of conversations that will be held over the life of each goal. These goals might surface in a long-term planning retreat or a yearly performance review. For example, Ben, a team leader, states the following global goal to his manager based on a mental model that he holds:

The B team is a long way from making decisions on their own. My goal is to get them to set more of their own goals and procedures. I also want them to self-monitor their progress in reaching their goals.

This goal is concerned with team self-management and is organized around two fundamental assumptions: first, groups are capable of leading themselves, particularly in areas such as goal setting, monitoring progress towards goals, setting expectations, and giving feedback and reinforcement. Second, the leader's role is to encourage the group's self-leadership. Clearly, such a complex goal will require a lot of time and many conversations.

Short-Term Goals

Global goals are usually achieved by accomplishing a series of *short-term goals*. The duration of short-term goals might be measured in months, weeks, or days, or even in specific meetings. Whatever their duration, they are the steps that allow us to achieve our global goals.

Short-term goals are often the subject of a single conversation and are preset before the conversation begins. For example, Ben, the team leader, relays a short-term goal to a team member:

My goal for our meeting on Monday will be to get the team to decide how they will manage their vacation schedule.

This vacation scheduling goal is a very concrete, specific goal. It reflects one step in realizing Ben's global goal of getting the team to make decisions on its own.

Emergent Goals

Not all of our communication goals are set prior to interaction. How many times have your initial goals for a conversation been modified and have new goals emerged once you and others began talking? Quite often, we suspect, because people frequently communicate in situations that are fast moving and fluid. In these situations, we communicate purposefully but not always consciously.

Sound confusing? It's not really, when you consider that we nearly always communicate with certain ideas in mind (and thus we are purposeful), but we are not always conscious of how we select and arrange our words.

The goals that pop up in our work conversations without our conscious planning or preparation are emergent goals. *Emergent goals* are set on the spot as intermediate goals in support of short-term or global goals (Wilson and Putnam, 1990). They emerge as we begin to speak to others and they speak to us. We send a message, they respond, we respond to their response, and so on. In social interaction, it is not always easy to predict what other people will say, how they will feel, or what new information they will introduce. By necessity, then, some of our goals do not emerge until talking begins.

Let's return to Ben to examine his emergent goals more thoroughly. He is discussing his short-term goal, the vacation policy, with Kathy, one of his direct reports.

Kathy: On this vacation schedule that the team has to get set up, I heard there may be a change with respect to seniority?

Ben: Well, to answer your question, I don't look for a change in policy. The team will have to approach that one just like they did for the safety issue.

Ben's response to Kathy reflects the setting of an emergent goal. Ben is mindful of his global goal around decision making and has recently set a short-term goal about vacation scheduling as a step toward the global goal. He is suddenly presented with another opportunity, and he is ready. He knows his direction even if he did not know ahead of time that he would have to answer the specific question posed.

As we said earlier, all three types of communication goals can either be global, short-term, or emergent. We might have a global relationship goal of increasing openness in a work relationship. This would be supported by a set of short-term goals and, when the opportunities strike, numerous emergent goals. Our short-term goals would be set by each occasion and the topics slated for discussion at anticipated meetings. Emergent goals, in turn, would be set as actual discussions proceed. They might lead to requests to share more specific information or to further explore feelings.

Identity goals may be broken down similarly. For example, as a manager, Carol was given a global identity goal by her manager, Bob, when he told her that she needed to raise her visibility in front of the plant manager. During meetings and plant tours with the plant manager, she was letting her work teams take all of the credit for the success of the unit, when she rightly deserved to be recognized. Because Bob felt this was hurting her career, he asked her to set a short-term goal of increasing her visibility during the next tour. He further suggested that she, rather than team members, discuss some of the unit's recent successes. As she answers some of the questions the plant manager is likely to pose, Carol will likely need to set some emergent identity goals.

Juggling Multiple Goals

We often find ourselves needing to manage more than one communication goal at a time. Global, short-term, and emergent goals do not operate independently of one another. Global goals structure short-term goals, and each of these can structure emergent goals (Wilson and Putnam, 1990). The process can also work in reverse. Emergent goals can cause a shift in goals that can reverberate back to the global level.

As just one example, when Dr. Barbara Barlow was first appointed chief of pediatric surgery at Harlem Hospital Center in the mid seventies, her global goals probably pertained to ensuring that the surgeries performed on children had successful outcomes (Hellman, 1995). But treating children who had fallen out of windows changed her outlook—and her goals. Over time, Barlow's goals expanded to encompass communicating prevention needs for the sorts of childhood injuries that brought children to the hospital emergency room. In addition to her responsibilities at the hospital, she advocated increasing the number of window gates in Harlem. Then she moved on to preventing other causes of trauma injuries to children, from unsafe playground equipment to unlit parks. She also helped to set up courses in street smarts and bicycle safety. Her emergent goals greatly altered both her global goals and her short-term goals, changing the fabric of her career.

Just as goals are linked on a time dimension (that is, global, short-term, and emergent), they are also often linked by their content and must be addressed simultaneously. For example, how often do you try to manage a specific impression of yourself when communicating about a task? How often are you concerned about not offending others or causing defensiveness as you discuss their performance or abilities? Do you measure your words when communicating politically sensitive information? If the answer to any of these questions is yes, then you have been juggling multiple communication goals. Your task is linked to your identity goal, your relationship goal, or both.

To really appreciate the nature of this juggling act, first consider a conversation that reflects only a single goal, a task goal. This conversation took place between Hillary, a young team leader fresh out of engineering school, and Herb, one of her team members. Herb was upset with the company for its policy of rotating new managers through the work team and saw Hillary as just the latest in a long line of new team leaders. Here is what transpired when Hillary sat down to talk with Herb.

Hillary: How can we improve around here, Herb?
   Herb: You want improvement? You get out there and learn the
            lines.

Poor Hillary! She was still figuring out where the bathrooms were when she had to bear the brunt of Herb's strong feelings about the company's policy for new managers. Herb's blunt, bold, in-your-face response was lacking in positive relationship and identity goals. Though he may have released some steam and achieved his task goal, Herb demonstrated a complete disregard for relationship or image building. If he was out to intimidate Hillary as well as change her behavior with regard to learning the lines, his communication strategy may reflect multiple goals. Either way, it made for an uncomfortable experience for Hillary.

A more constructive response for Herb would have been to focus on the problem without implying that Hillary is to blame, perhaps as follows:

Herb: I understand the position you are in as a manager. But
         from where I sit, the system needs improving. It seems to
         pit managers and team members against one another. Man-
         agers who rotate through this team need more training, or
         they'll continue to get in the way of our team's functioning.

Think how much more progress Hillary, Herb, and the entire team might have made if Herb had kept relationship and identity goals in mind.

Now let's consider a conversation in which multiple goals are clearly held. This is a conversation between Carolyn, the manager, and Sheila, a technician who reports to her. They are discussing a proposed opportunity for Sheila to become a trainer for Total Quality Management.

Speaker	Dialogue	Explanation
Carolyn	*When Bob told me that he was giving you the opportunity to go to the TQM training, I was really excited. And then we got to discussing it further, and the opportunity was to become the TQM trainer for our unit. And I wasn't sure that it fit. Not because you're not the person with all the energy to make it work.*	Carolyn manages her own identity as excited. Carolyn manages Sheila's identity and saves face.
Sheila	*Mm-hmm.*	
Carolyn	*But with all the stuff that you need to be doing, a week out right now is critical. If you come back and tell me that you definitely want to be the trainer, I'll say okay.*	Carolyn manages the relationship by offering Sheila a choice.
Sheila	*Mm-hmm.*	
Carolyn	*But I'm concerned.*	Carolyn manages her own identity as concerned.

This conversation tells us that Carolyn had three broad goals. First and foremost, she had a task goal, which was to influence

Sheila to choose the TQM training at another time. Carolyn also pursued a relationship goal and an identity goal. Her relationship goal was to help Sheila save face; she managed this by communicating that Sheila's availability, not her competence to be a TQM trainer, is at issue. Carolyn's identity goal was to maintain the correct image of herself as a manager.

The status and power differences imposed by the hierarchical nature of most organizations is one reason that we hold multiple goals. Further complicating the power dynamics are differences due to factors such as race, gender, age, education, and socioeconomic status. There are also individual differences in competence, experience, and overall professional attractiveness. All of these potential differences influence how level the playing field is between communicators. The more level the playing field, the more negotiable the task. To the degree the playing field is not level, the leader's view of the task often predominates, while employees feel obligated to show deference. Thus, relationship goals frequently affect how the task is defined and completed.

In our example, Sheila offered little resistance to Carolyn's desire to delay Sheila's participation in the training. Sheila may have truly concurred with Carolyn that this was a busy time, but Sheila may also have felt powerless to negotiate her manager's marked preference. If this is true, someone on a more equal footing with Carolyn might have negotiated an earlier access to the training opportunity. Often, the question comes down to which goals are to be met and in what order. In juggling multiple goals and increasing the likelihood of meeting them, it is often useful to first focus on the goals themselves.

Goal Analysis

Over twenty years ago, Robert Mager (1972) introduced a technique called goal analysis, the purpose of which was to define one's goals and make them tangible. The logic of a goal analysis is to narrow the set of possible meanings for a broad goal and thus pave a more direct path to goal achievement. The process is a good one to more clearly define our task, relationship, and identity communication goals—and to know when we might do better to keep our statements of goals slightly ambiguous.

Performances and Fuzzies

Mager distinguished between performances and fuzzies. *Performances* help to define in more specific terms what we mean by our important but often abstract goals. They name the essential aspects of our general goal statements. In contrast, *fuzzies* are goal statements that retain an abstract vague quality. "Communicate that I do good work," is considered a fuzzy because many types of performances would qualify as good work. However, "Communicate that I consistently meet my sales quota" is a performance. "Retain my autonomy" is considered a fuzzy because of the numerous ways one could retain autonomy; in contrast, "Refuse help from my boss on the XYZ project" is a performance.

A performance does not have to involve external behaviors only. There are internal performances, such as those involving thinking or feeling. "Be happy" is a fuzzy, because it doesn't tell you how to be happy. One internal performance for it might be, "See the positive aspects of situations rather than the negative aspects."

Mager (1972, p. 28) suggests that the best way to tell the difference between a performance and a fuzzy is to ask, "Is there a single behavior or class of behaviors that will indicate the presence of an alleged performance, about which there would be general agreement?" If the answer to the question is no, then you have a fuzzy goal. If the answer is yes, you have identified a performance goal.

When Ambiguity Is Intentional

But are fuzzies always a bad thing? Just how specific do we need to be about our communication goals? Today, we would answer these questions a little bit differently than when Mager was writing in the 1970s. Historically, in the United States, we have equated specificity with effective communication and vagueness or ambiguity with ineffective communication. In *The Art of Japanese Management,* Richard Pascale and Anthony Athos (1981, p. 102) addressed this point, noting the differences between American and Japanese management cultures: "Explicit communication is a cultural assumption; it is not a linguistic imperative. Skilled executives develop the ability to vary their language along the spectrum from explicitness to indirection depending upon their reading of the other person and the situation."

There is no doubt that many of the situations we encounter do require specificity. For example, we have a set of industry standards or government regulations that must be followed to the letter. Or we have a specific quality or background experience that we want others to know about because it pertains to a task or a relationship. Or we must deliver negative performance feedback to an employee, and for the feedback to be useful, we need to specify what the other person has done wrong. In these situations, vague communication goals can lead to a fuzzy framing of the issues, which, in turn, may produce confusion and misunderstanding.

However, there are also situations where the use of ambiguity is strategic and effective. Lest you think fuzzies are bad form all of the time, consider that ambiguity can actually help in negotiating conflict situations, communicating expectations, and managing organizational change (Pascale and Athos, 1981; Eisenberg, 1984).

Ambiguous language can help in conflict situations and preserve strained relationships. Explicit acknowledgement of a hopeless impasse can end a conversation when ambiguous language might preserve the opening for options not yet discovered. Explicit language assessing blame or fault can cause people to lose face so that they may find it impossible to continue in the relationship. When people with very different values must work together, broad ambiguous statements of unit goals may allow them to see these goals as compatible with their own.

In circumstances where greater participation is of value, managers are increasingly inclined to name a desired outcome or goal with the least amount of specificity necessary to meet overall organizational needs. This enables employees to decide how to achieve the desired outcome; the employees are more empowered, and the organization benefits from the creative alternatives generated.

As one example, the second author of this book (Bob Sarr) was in charge of a railcar renovation project for Santa Fe Southern Railway that worked precisely in this fashion. The goal was to create a venue that offered the option of upscale elegance and yet day-to-day serviceability for a variety of uses. Employees generated a wide variety of possibilities that no one in management had considered.

Elegance, budget, and serviceability were served well beyond the expectations of owners.

Finally, ambiguous language and generally framed goals often help facilitate organizational change. Ambiguous goals can help when a decision to take specific action would be premature, yet communicating a general concern for the issue commits people to act without naming a specific course of action (Pascale and Athos, 1981). For example, when one organization shifted its traditionally managed plants to team-based systems, its leaders communicated a general goal of shifting from a job-based system to a cross-functional team-based system. They then let each site have great latitude as to the final organizational design and process for change.

Moreover, organizations that adopt central metaphors (such as the family metaphor) to help their members define or redefine organizational life promote what Eisenberg (1984, pp. 232–233) calls a unified diversity of interpretations. Of the family metaphor he says, "Individuals believe that they agree on what it means to be a part of a 'family,' yet the actual interpretations remain quite different." The attitudes of both "all forgiving" and "tough love" fall within the spectrum of the meanings for family.

The point is that you must ask yourself the question, "How specific should my various communication goals be, given the situation?" On the one hand, if the costs of misunderstanding, confusion, and divergent interpretations are too great, then the fuzziness needs to be reduced. To do that, identify all possible performances and ask of each one, "If someone achieved or demonstrated each of these performances, would I be willing to say he (or she) has achieved the goal?" When the answer is yes, the goal has been narrowed. On the other hand, when a diversity of interpretations or independent and creative solutions to problems are needed, then stating goals in broad general terms is quite appropriate.

Why We Need Good Mental Models

To this point, we have focused almost exclusively on describing the nature of the communication goals that individuals hold in terms of their content, scope and duration over time, and level of specificity. We now turn to the role of mental models in goal formation.

Mental models influence our goal setting because the dimensions of our model direct what we pay attention to and what we ignore. Often our mental models set up an ideal, a standard, or an exemplary case that we use to compare against current circumstances. When we are reminded of our mental model in attempting to understand a new situation, we formulate a goal congruent with our model if the situation matches our model. If we are reminded of a mental model, but the situation is not a perfect match for it, we still use the model but adapt it to the situation and set our goals.

As proof of this, answer the questions set forth in Questionnaire 2.1 as completely as possible. Also, note mentally to yourself whether you have a lot or a little to say regarding each question.

Questionnaire 2.1. Identifying Mental Models.

1. To which of the following positive qualities would you say, "That's me!"?

Independent	Passionate
Intelligent	Risk Taking
Generous	Loving
Assertive	Witty
Strong-Willed	Articulate
Healthy	Wise

   What other positive qualities would you attribute to yourself? What negative qualities would you attribute to yourself?

2. What epitomizes your idea of an effective leader?

3. What is the purpose of your unit in relation to the overall function of the organization?

4. How would you like your company/unit to look in five years? in ten years?

5. What principles really matter to you? What do you stand for?

6. What really counts in your organization? What does it take to get ahead?

7. What "scripts" do you follow when you conduct a formal job interview, performance appraisal, or staff meeting?

8. What "scripts" do you follow when you enter a restaurant, go to a religious or spiritual gathering, or attend a sporting event?

If you can answer the questions posed in Questionnaire 2.1, and we suspect that you can easily answer most of them, then you have shown that you have mental models for yourself (Question 1) and for the leadership roles that you or others play (Question 2). You have mental models for the mission of your work unit (Question 3), an organizational vision (Question 4), and a set of values for yourself (Question 5) and your organization (Question 6). Finally, you have mental models for a variety of situations at work and outside of work (Questions 7 and 8). These models comprise a set of script-like sequences of behaviors that we follow, such as the greeting, question-answer, and closing phases of a job interview.

Imagine that your boss begins a discussion of a new business venture by asking you how much of a risk taker you are. If you answered "That's me!" to this item in Question 1, then the communication goal you set to describe yourself would be congruent with your mental model, prompting you to utter words to that effect.

Perhaps you are new to a company and witness a young manager in your charge making an inappropriate sexual advance to one of the department secretaries. While you may not be fully aware of the specifics of the company's sexual harassment policy because of your newness, you might, on the spot, use your combined mental models for an effective leader (Question 2), your values (Question 5), and the organization's values (Question 6) to formulate a goal to alter the young manager's behavior and attitudes.

Suppose you found yourself unprepared for several questions asked of you in a recent job interview. When a colleague asks you how things went, you would use your mental model for a good job interview (Question 7) and indicate that your performance lacked the necessary preparation.

As these examples show, situations can fully or partly match our mental models; either scenario enables us to use the models to formulate appropriate goals. But what if you had comparatively little to say when you answered the questions in Questionnaire 2.1? Take Question 6, for example. Suppose you recently started a new job, and you did not know specifically what it took to get ahead in the organization. Under these circumstances, your mental model would be considered weak because it would be poorly developed. Just how much of a drawback is a poorly developed mental model?

Put yourself in the shoes of a young manager at a bank branch who was responsible for a teller who, according to other tellers, began "acting strangely" on the job and making mistakes at the teller window (Fairhurst, Green, and Snavely, 1984). This manager had several futile talks with the employee to better understand her strange behavior, since he had not observed it himself. Here is what he said when he finally discovered that the source of her problem was epilepsy.

> My tellers told me on a couple of occasions that she would act strange. That could mean a lot of things, okay? Generally speaking, the acting strange would be just kind of staring out in space, like she wasn't there, not knowing what was going on around her.
>
> We called the city life squad one afternoon, and they came and took her to the hospital. She was released that night and was back to work the next day happy, joking with the tellers, just as though nothing had happened. I called her into my office, and she did not volunteer the information that she was epileptic. I had to ask her directly and at that point she confirmed it. I sent her on over to the teller window then, and she ran it just fine. At that point, I think I realized that some of these blank stares, those lost feelings were because she was on the verge of going, and she could control it. She didn't know where she was for a minute or two, and then she came back. It was during some of these periods that she created mistakes in her work and had no idea why there was a mistake. It was because she wasn't even there, didn't even know what happened.

For several days, the manager did not have a clear picture—a mental model—for this teller's behavior. All he knew was that the teller was acting strangely, and that the other tellers and customers were turning to him for answers to this puzzle. Yet he could not respond until his own picture was clear, until he had clarified his mental model of the situation.

Once he had formed his mental model, in a surprise move, he sought to terminate the teller. He reasoned that epilepsy was the cause of the mistakes she was making at the teller window, and the mistakes were costing the bank money. Some employees, however, felt that the manager's action was extreme and that there was other work at the bank that the teller could do. But the manager's model apparently did not include the option of reassigning individuals who were not able to be tellers.

As we begin to accumulate experiences in an unfamiliar arena, we form new models; thus, new models are based on limited experience. Since greater complexity in our models tends to moderate our judgments (Fiske and Taylor, 1991), the manager's termination of the epileptic employee is easily understood in light of the newness and, hence, simplicity of his model. Given more experience with epileptics, this manager's dealings with the epileptic employee might have been more informed. He would have known that this dysfunction can vary in severity, and he would have understood how helpful medication can be. He might not have acted so quickly to terminate and might have considered other options based upon further details about the extent of the teller's medical condition. The more varied our experience with others, the less extreme our judgments.

If we are to communicate as we should and not mismanage meaning, we must be mindful of the responsibility to develop our mental models and to revise them as we become more experienced. For example, we must guard against a tendency to blame an unidentified amorphous "they" for making life tough in the organization—or elsewhere. Even those high up in an organization and those seen to be most powerful can always look upward or outward and find someone else who is making life difficult. Whether it is the senior manager from the "old school," the intransigent board of directors, the cranky customers, or some agency of government, there will always be a "they."

We must recognize that everyone operates from different sets of needs and pressing demands. We do ourselves and those demands no good if we simply feel sorry for ourselves. If we stop thinking and trying to understand others' perspectives and needs, we stop developing our mental models to handle arguments and counterarguments.

The second author of this book (Bob Sarr), in the early stages of consulting with a European division of an American consumer goods company, noticed that many of the top managers in the European subsidiaries did a lot of "poor us" complaining. In one conversation, he pointedly asked, "What are your potential competitive strengths as this company's European organization?" Not one of the six individuals in the room could come up with an answer. Their self-defeating and destructive mental model had become a basis for "poor us" framing throughout the organization.

His question literally stopped the conversation cold and, had it not been for outside prodding, their destructive mental model would have continued to impede future progress.

What Are the Components of a Good Mental Model?

The bank branch manager and the European managers discussed above had underdeveloped mental models characterized by simplifying assumptions, the chief consequences of which were distorted judgment and poorly set communication goals. When our mental models are complex, they comprise an interrelated set of beliefs that go together in some way; they are "theory-like" (Senge, 1990). As the experiential basis of the model becomes richer, dimensions are added and connected to one another (Fiske and Taylor, 1991). Managers who are known as good coaches or mentors, for example, often become that way because their rich experiences of dealing with people produce more complexity, which translates to more "linkages" in their mental models. As a result, they read people better and can thus respond more effectively.

Here is a typical example from a manager who is known as a good coach. He is describing one of his team members.

> I got a natural leader on my team—very verbal, can argue any point from any direction, any time depending on what mood he is in. He can be very influential.
>
> He's a contributor mostly, unless he's in a bad mood. Then he's like lightning in a bottle. You have no idea where he'll direct his fire or what he'll say. It's strange, I know, but he can do damage. When he's in one of his moods, I table issues, cut the meeting short, and then talk sense into him the next day, when it's all blown over.

This manager's description suggests two different but related mental models. The first hint of a mental model occurs when the manager describes his team member as a "natural leader," who is "very verbal" and "very influential." No doubt this manager has run across natural leaders before who were verbally skilled. His mental model applies to types of individuals—in this case, natural leaders.

But the manager also reveals a mental model more specific to this team member. He draws from a more general "natural leader" model, because the team member's behavior reminded him of it. But he also adds to it the team member's less desirable qualities, the capacity to be "lightning in a bottle" and "do damage." Together, they form a set of interrelated beliefs that hang together for the manager in a way that helps him to know how to respond, especially when the team member's mood turns ugly.

Each dimension or linkage in our mental model is critical to helping us understand new situations because of the phenomenon of *reminding*. Reminding is at the root of understanding; to understand something new means finding something in our memory to relate to it (Riesbeck and Schank, 1989). Each experience in a given area adds to our knowledge in ways that allow us both to see patterns and interrelationships and to recognize anomalies, exceptions to the rule, and the like. The more refined the knowledge stored in our memory, the more there is to be reminded of and the better able are we to make sense of a situation and formulate the appropriate goal to respond.

From a mental modeling perspective, we can now see why today's leaders are urged to develop a vision for the future, a clear mission, and a strong set of values. These items reflect what Peter Senge calls a set of "governing ideas" that answer the critical questions of what, why, and how.

- What is the picture of the future—the vision—that we seek to create?

- Why do we exist? Or, put another way, what is our purpose or mission? A sense of purpose that is larger than simply the needs of shareholders and employees enables the organization to contribute to the world in some unique way.

- How do we want to act, consistent with our mission, along the path toward achieving our vision? A company's core values (perhaps integrity, openness, honesty, freedom, equal opportunity, leanness, merit, or loyalty) describe how the company wants life to be on a day-to-day basis, while pursuing the vision [1990, pp. 223–224].

These ideas govern by virtue of the reminding properties of mental models. When leaders develop mental models for mission, values, and vision, they are reminded of them in day-in and day-out problem solving and so act with them in mind to help make them a reality. A clear mission will help focus energies and promote a wise use of resources because leaders are reminded of what is and is not central to the organization. Values define what really matters in the organization and remind leaders of the standards to strive for in trying to realize the mission and vision. Finally, vision supplies a specific direction to pursue and reminds leaders that the choices made today are precisely what brings about tomorrow's future.

Our mental models for these governing ideas gain in complexity when each idea is fitted to the circumstances in which we must lead and when the interrelationships between the ideas are clearly seen. The capacity to be reminded of our mission, vision, and values in the midst of what can sometimes be all-consuming problems is often half the battle in figuring out the correct response. It enables us to remain true to who we are as an organization and what we're about.

Leaders who develop their mental models for mission, vision, and values are able to formulate clear and consistent communication goals to articulate them. This chapter concludes with an example of one leader who was able to do exactly this.

Mental Models and Managing Meaning Through Framing

In Chapter One, we presented a conversation between Don, a team leader, who shared with Sally his image of team functioning. Here, we will review that conversation, this time focusing on how Don uses his mental models in his talk with Sally.

Speaker	Dialogue	Explanation
(1) Don	*But people seem to operate as if they're very restricted, and that's not right. The way that plays out is people want a lot of strong, clear direction.*	Because of Don's mental model regarding a vision for his unit and the values implied by it, he framed the team's direction seeking as "not right."
(2) Sally	*Yeah.*	

Speaker	Dialogue	Explanation
(3) Don	*But I have a picture of the process I want this team-based organization to follow. And one of the things that I am consciously choosing not to do is to give direction, because I want us to struggle a little bit. I know that it is a struggle for the organization. I've offered a couple suggestions about possible goals for the future but I have not prescribed that yet. The way I tend to operate is, if we are in some kind of crisis mode, as was often the case in my last job, then I am prescriptive if necessary. I would say frequently, "Here's what we have to do."*	Also because of his vision, he took exception to the team's direction seeking and framed opposite behaviors, such as "not give direction" and "struggle."
(4)	*My sense is that we're not in a crisis mode, so we have ample time and opportunity for in-volvement, participation, wrestling with the issues, and being a little frus-trated with why we're not where we want to be. And my desire is that we, as a group, would say,*	Because Don's recent job experience was contrary to his mental model for crisis situations, he framed this job experience as "not in a crisis mode."

Speaker	Dialogue	Explanation
	"Hey, we are just not happy with where we are. We want to do something about that." And I'm waiting on our module to decide that.	
(5) Sally	*I see what you are saying.*	
(6) Don	*This is very different for me. So one of the things that I keep telling myself is that this is a learning experience of being in a role that's a not a crisis situation and giving the organization the space it needs.*	Because of Don's mental model as it relates to his role in noncrisis situations, he framed his purpose as "giving the organization the space it needs."
(7) Sally	*Mm-hmm.*	
(8) Don	*I get frustrated when people come in and talk with me on this project or that project, whatever it is, people are really looking for me to give them an answer.*	
(9) Sally	*The right answer* [laughs].	
(10) Don	*The right answer* [laughs]. *Since I have a lot of history of doing that, I'm still trying to be patient, but it is hard work because a part of me likes being in the driver's seat.*	Finally, because of Don's mental model for himself, he framed one of his qualities as "likes being in the driver's seat."
(11) Sally	*What you are doing is clearly different from*	

Speaker	Dialogue	Explanation
	previous leaders, previous managers. Actually, we haven't had many leaders. We have had managers, which would be the more directive-type person. And you are right; people have gotten used to that.	

In this conversation, we can see how several of Don's mental models come into play. He used a mental model for his vision of desired team functioning, one for crisis situations to indicate that they were not in a crisis mode, one to spell out his role in noncrisis situations, and one of himself when he said he "likes being in the driver's seat."

Well-developed mental models for mission, vision, and values must fit the circumstances in which we lead. Don understood the importance of this point: he went beyond simply accepting the company's vision of self-managing teams and developed his own mental model of a self-managing team in his team's specific circumstances. Note what Don said in this regard: "And one of the things that I am consciously choosing not to do is to give direction, because I want us to struggle a little bit" *(3)*.

The company vision provides only the context and overall direction for the local vision. Nowhere did the corporate vision mention the need to struggle. Without Don's vision of less direction and more struggle in this local context, the company vision fails. Don had to step forward and ground the company vision based on his experiences, what he knew to be true in this work setting, and what he knew to be important for his people. Regardless of where we are in the hierarchy, we must develop our own specific mental models in order to lead. The mental model must fit our circumstances.

Moreover, to be so clear about the direction he wants his team to go in, Don must be very clear about its purpose. He knows exactly why team members are here and what role his unit plays in the overall functioning of the plant.

Finally, from Don's statement about desired team functioning *(3)*, we know that Don clearly values participation for teams. It is another reason why Don calls attention to the apparent restrictiveness of the team's behavior and then goes on to place a value judgment on it by framing it as not right *(1)*. This is a prime example of the interrelatedness of vision, mission, and values and one reason some use the terms *corporate philosophy* or *credo* instead.

Each of Don's mental models is fairly detailed and developed enough to present a clear image from which to work. The clearer the image, the more consistently can we use it as an internal guideline in evaluating new situations. Our communication goals are more likely to be clear and consistent as we manage meaning across situations because we are using the same internal point of reference each time.

As demonstrated by the case of the bank branch manager who responded to the teller's strange behavior, poorly defined mental models based on images that are blurry or indistinct can make for simplifying assumptions that lead to distorted judgment and ineffective communication goals. As the case of the European managers demonstrated, however, mental models can also be based on relatively clear but incorrect assumptions that similarly produce the wrong communication goals. In the next chapter, we examine one way to avoid such problems. We will learn ways to bring mental models to the surface for some critical and productive examination.

A Backward Glance at This Chapter

This chapter focused on how our mental models help us to make sense of situations and formulate our goals for communicating, including what and how we choose to frame. We learned the components of good mental models and how they support the management of meaning. To recap briefly:

- Our communication goals vary by content: they may be focused on task, relationship, or identity.
- Our communication goals vary by time duration: they may be global, short term, or emergent.
- Our communication goals vary in specificity. At certain times, ambiguity is useful; at other times, we need absolute clarity.

- Mental models play a crucial role in goal formation because they create a standard, an ideal, or an exemplary case with which to make sense of a situation and formulate a goal.
- Good mental models have many dimensions and linkages that we can be reminded of in new situations.
- Mission, vision, and values are the components of good mental models for leaders. The power of a mental model lies in its fit to the circumstances and in clearly drawn interrelationships.
- Mental models help set consistent communication goals because the same internal point of reference is used to manage meaning across many situations.

Now, having seen the importance of mental models generally, in Chapter Three we turn our attention to how to best develop our mental models as leaders.

Vision-Based Framing
Enabling People to See the World You See

A meaningful vision charts a future path that is based on a well-defined mission, or purpose, and a clear set of values. Visions are central to leadership success because of their transforming power. Shared visions transform individuals "from robots blindly following instructions to human beings engaged in a creative and purposeful venture" (Bennis and Nanus, 1985, p. 91). An organizational vision is not a terribly complex notion in theory, yet the unfortunate reality is that much is lost in practice. People need skills, which often remain undeveloped and untapped, to do the framing necessary to translate the vision's general and sometimes abstract ideas into specific, practical ones.

We begin this chapter by exploring the day-to-day demands of framing for vision. We show what happened when one organization that we have studied introduced W. Edwards Deming's Total Quality Management (TQM) to realize its corporate vision; we then point out lessons that can be learned from its experience. Later in the chapter, we show you how to meet the everyday demands of framing your vision through the development of your mental models.

Coordinating Vision and Frame

Recently, the first author of this book (Gail Fairhurst) worked with an organization during its companywide communications audit. As part of the audit, employees were given an opportunity to rewrite the stated vision to reflect what they believed to be the real vision. A significant number of workers chose to undertake this task and pointed out a clear contradiction: the stated vision was for workers to work themselves out of a job as soon as possible because they were involved in a plant shutdown; the real vision, according to many workers, was to delay this as long as possible. The audit also showed that few managers ever explicitly talked about the vision of the organization, thus leaving it vulnerable to those who would pursue their own interests. Managers, of course, knew the company vision but were unable to align operations—behavior, policies, and practices—with the vision's sentiments.

Like corporate philosophy statements of any kind, vision statements are, of necessity, quite general in nature. In fact, a number of ambiguous communication goals might be strategically formulated. Their aim is to promote a unified diversity of interpretations (Eisenberg, 1984); that is, be pliable enough that a range of different organizational functions can apply the goals to their situation yet still hold true to the basic ideas. But all too often, many managers don't apply the vision. Instead, they come to regard it with indifference or cynicism, as do those who report to them. Why is this so? There are several answers.

- The vision may not be well formulated.
- People have not taken time to develop mental models for the vision.
- People have not been taught how to communicate a vision.

As we will see, even one of these causes may provide insurmountable roadblocks to realizing the vision. Or the causes may pile up on one another. But these roadblocks can be removed, and a path to realizing the vision can be cleared.

- *A vision must be well formulated.* As we have seen, a meaningful vision charts a future path that is based on a clear purpose and set of values. If either the future path, organizational purpose, or key values are not well-understood parts of the vision statement, vision rhetoric serves no useful purpose.

George Bush's run at a second term in office and his portrayal of himself as "the managerial president" provide testimony to the real importance of vision. During the 1988 election, Bush was widely mocked by the press for his reference to "the vision thing." More manager than leader, George Bush was thought to lack both a vision and an understanding of its necessity. Although the word *vision* was prominent in the rhetoric of his 1992 campaign, Bush aides were reported to be very nervous whenever Bush was asked about his plans for a second term. His response, "I'll handle whatever comes up" (Klein, 1992), again indicated a lack of vision and a subsequent inability to frame the future in very concrete terms. He blindly assumed that the electorate would·fill in the blanks about his ability to address the future and dealt his campaign a severe blow in the process.

• *Managers need time to develop their mental models for an organizational vision.* Bell Atlantic CEO and chairman of the board Raymond Smith discovered the need for time to develop mental models when he was moving about the company before he became CEO. He was struck by how few people understood the actions of the corporation, on any scale, whether the purchase of a new business or the consolidation of an operations center (Kanter, 1991). Even when employees understood their own objectives and those of the department in which they worked, they missed out on the big picture. Smith took this to heart, saying,

"When 99 percent of someone's efforts are engaged in getting a departmental job done, the broad goals of the corporation begin to fade if they are not constantly reinforced. As head coach and teacher, I hadn't really taught the game plan or the course well enough. So I went on the stump, enlisted the aid of a number of others and spread the word" (p. 125).

As part of spreading the word, Smith asked four hundred top managers to take the time to understand and internalize (that is, develop their mental models for) Bell Atlantic's purpose, vision, and overall strategy. After what he describes as a "brief hiccup" in the company while these ideas were being absorbed, things took off. These four hundred managers were able to communicate clearly and personally to thousands of other Bell Atlantic employees by translating personal and departmental objectives to those of the company. As a result of the process, Smith felt that the company became better able deal with the tough realities it faced. Bell Atlantic's emergence as an entrepreneurial innovator bears out his conclusion.

• *Managers must be taught how to communicate a vision.* In the implementation of many visions, one person's view of the future is imposed on others; the visions are, in the parlance of one organization we studied, "lay-ons." Yet for a vision to energize and unite others toward a common purpose, it must be shared. Unfortunately, many managers do not yet know the importance of sharing the vision, nor have they seen it demonstrated in the day-to-day workings of their organizations. The first step in achieving a shared vision is a willingness to communicate with others about the vision's fit into the local context.

Too often managers fail to acknowledge that problems and new situations constantly call into question the relevance of the vision. Organizational visions must be continuously formulated and reformulated to ensure the necessary links between vision, mission, and operations (Hitt, Keats, Harback, and Nixon, 1994). Moreover, if we are going to frame well, our vision must provide a picture into which others can insert themselves. Companywide visions often fail in this regard because their role is to provide only the context and direction for a local vision. A local vision must be focused, clearly related to our specific unit or function, and detailed enough to assist in the day-in and day-out problem solving of those with whom we work. It is with these visions that a better future can be realized.

Local Realities of Communicating a Corporate Vision

We learned the need for good framing at the local level when we had the opportunity to examine close-up the everyday realities of communicating and implementing a new corporate program. The vision of the company was to become a highly customer-responsive low-cost producer of a set of household products, using semi-autonomous team-based systems. Toward this end, senior management promoted W. Edwards Deming's Total Quality Management as a program that provided a set of tools and a way of thinking necessary to realize the vision.

The company used a variety of methods to get the initial word out, including numerous training opportunities, newsletters and senior management speeches devoted to TQM, and appointments of TQM coordinators for every site. They even had frequent appearances by Deming himself. The task of the authors of this book was to tape-record conversations in the offices and shop floors of the company, away from the hoopla of internal corporate campaigns and at the points where day-to-day work took place.

As we learned, TQM was put under intense scrutiny by the workforce because of some fundamental needs they possessed. We had a chance to chronicle those needs and see how managers responded to them. The conversations we monitored and report here are about TQM; yet we have found that any new vision or program faces similar trials. Indeed, we suggest that these are fundamental needs of organizational members.

Understand the New Ideas

We heard many conversations in which the primary objective was to make sense of TQM. This need to understand the new ideas would seem to be obvious, but not all managers recognized it. Some managers saw the raising of problems with TQM as opportunities to further the goal of explaining it; others missed these opportunities completely. Managers who do not shy away from problem-oriented discussions find that attempts to resolve the predicaments reveal the choices that exist with respect to vision or program adoption (Hosking and Morley, 1988).

Here is a good example. Jocelyn has questions about Deming's statistical process control and its various charting procedures. In sharing her questions with Marshall, her TQM coordinator for the plant, she reveals a choice over whether to use a pareto or a control chart.

> *Jocelyn:* I'm just trying to understand. If I looked at a pareto chart or a bar chart or a pie chart or whatever, what would I want to be seeing with that chart? If something like this says we're trending, we're staying the same—
>
> *Marshall:* You would have to see a different pareto or pie chart every week.
>
> *Jocelyn:* I'm not sure what that would tell me different than what the control chart already tells me. Have you thought that through?
>
> *Marshall:* No, I didn't think through that.

Jocelyn: You don't want to chart just for charting's sake. And there may be something relevant there that I'm missing.

Marshall: No, you're right. The charts are not time dependent. A pareto, a pie chart, or any one of those charts do not show trends over time.

Notice that Jocelyn's questions to Marshall require answers that make explicit the assumptions of the particular charting method in question. Jocelyn and Marshall conclude that Deming's other charting methods add little beyond what the control charting already provides. Jocelyn is clear that any new set of ideas requires them to thoughtfully select from among the offerings. She can see and help Marshall to see where the fit lies between their work and the Deming tools.

To make good use of problems or predicaments, we must commit to exploring possible solutions or means to a solution. In the following example, Bob, the plant manager, and Fred, one of his group managers, discuss only the problem. The conversation goes no further.

Bob: He sent me this chart, okay?

Fred: I'll never understand all these charts.

Bob: [*Laughs.*] That one where they did the fishbone exercise gave me heartburn. I told Mark, our trainer, it gave me heartburn. I'm not sure he appreciated it.

After Fred expresses his problem, Bob changes the subject to a discussion of work teams and does not return to the issue of charting in the ensuing thirty-minute conversation. They get on with the business at hand but never address Fred's difficulty with the charts.

Yet, because of his position in the organization, Bob has a greater formal responsibility to advocate for TQM than does Fred. Bob must be committed to addressing this and other problems—and to helping Fred do so with others. At a minimum, this could mean finding someone who could help them understand the charts. In this instance, Bob missed an opportunity to clarify the kinds of information that TQM charts can provide. Instead of using the predicament to drive change at this juncture, through his own inertia and lack of understanding, Bob allowed a gap in understanding to continue. If too many moments like this accumulate, new ideas have no chance.

See How the New Ideas Are Relevant to One's Job

Understanding a set of new ideas is no guarantee they will be useful; for this, they must be personalized and made relevant to recurring responsibilities. Once again, the problems or predicaments raised often provide the opportunity for personalizing the new ideas. In the following dialogue, Carl presents just such a problem to his manager, Nate, which prompts Nate to try to personalize the TQM vision for Carl.

Carl: On this TQM thing, I really struggled with that at the meeting—to figure out how this TQM fits with my project on downsizing. If it doesn't contribute to the quality of the project or the product we put out in this plant, why even mess with it, okay?

Nate: What are we providing? We're not making product. You're not; I'm not. Okay?

Carl: The plant is.

Nate: Yeah, the plant is, but you and I indirectly are. Remember the fundamental TQM questions. Who are your customers? Would it be manufacturing, accounting, engineering? The answer is everybody that will utilize energy in the future. Okay, what do they need? What's your product or service? Not the plant's—your product or service? Their needs are to have a cheap source of energy to be able to make their products.

Carl's predicament is over TQM's perceived lack of relevance to his project, which is to provide cheaper steam, water, and utilities to the manufacturing lines and support functions in the plant. It is very clear that Carl is ready to abandon TQM unless its relevance to his role can be demonstrated. Nate embarks on a set of questions designed to clarify the meaning of TQM for work units that do not directly manufacture product and do not see the typical view of a consumer as applying to their "users." Nate reframes the notion of customers, shifting from the plant's frame of customers as consumers of a product to a more general frame of customers as consumers of the member's services. By framing in this way, he defines a new class of customers and makes TQM actionable, because the questions of quality and improvement directed at plant customer activities also apply to Carl's customers, just in different ways.

Feel the Enthusiasm of Others, Especially One's Boss, Toward the New Ideas

No matter how great people think an idea is, they are not likely to pursue it with much enthusiasm if their bosses or others they depend upon for support are indifferent or disapproving. By demonstrating real enthusiasm for the new ideas, leaders can create a safe space to release others' interest in the ideas.

We were struck by a conversation between Pete, a department manager, and Ken, one of his team leaders, because of its potential for helping Ken feel his boss's enthusiasm toward TQM. In this conversation, Pete and Ken are talking about how Ken's team is likely to respond to TQM's statistical processes and charting methods. As you read the following excerpt, pay particular attention to Pete's language.

Pete: We gotta do a lotta managin' around it though, Ken. I mean just manage the hell out of it. If they had their way, they would be out there for eight hours, exchange whatever information they needed to, and then leave. There would be no attempt to consolidate, review, or make sense of the information. So we have got to reinforce it—kill it with them.

Ken: Oh yeah.

Pete: I mean every time we talk to them.

Ken: Sure, we must make sure they know it's there and they're gonna use it.

Pete: Right!

Ken: And if they don't want to use it, at least come and ask, "Hey, I got a problem here. What can I do about it?" I'll say, "Have you checked the book? Have you checked your process audit book?" And if they haven't, I'll tell them, "Well, let's go look at it." If we can get them to use the things that are in place, I think they can help themselves a lot more than they are doing right now.

There is a motivational quality to this exchange not unlike a coach's pep talk before a big game. Pete, the "coach" (manager) in this case, advises Ken of the problems that he will face with the team and how they need to be overcome. Note the intensity of Pete's language when he frames proposed actions that Ken might take and his repetition of his message about managing the team through their resistance.

Pete's goal—to support Ken in his advocacy of TQM with the team—is clearly apparent. His coaching style told Ken to expect resistance, be prepared for it, and enthusiastically fight it—which Ken seems ready to do. Pete infuses this conversation with an energy that, in essence, tells Ken to manage with vigor. It is no surprise, then, when Ken enthusiastically reinforces Pete's message to the point of supplying actual words and strategies that would overcome team member resistance.

See How the Ideas Fit with Established Programs and Practices

People are driven to make sense of new ideas by relating them to old ideas that form the basis of mental models. Are the new ideas a rejection of the old? Are they somehow related? In what ways?

Many of the problems raised with TQM were concerned with how it fit with established policies or programs. People needed to figure out ways to understand it, based upon their old models. One conversation over fit occurred when R. J., a manufacturing manager, went to a meeting at headquarters and gathered some information that caused him to question how TQM and the company's diversity policies meshed. He addressed his question to his manager, Jan. Here is what they said.

R. J.: In the monthly cultural meeting that I've just come back from, I heard the women talking in that group that the work teams in which they participated were filled with people who were giving their best effort, but that on the teams in which they were the only woman, they felt a sense of withdrawal because they didn't have another woman there for reinforcement or support. So, my question is, how does TQM match up with the diversity concerns that we have in this company?

Jan: Well, to my knowledge, TQM doesn't have a lot to say directly about diversity—but certainly Deming's points

about investing in people and driving out fear are very
consistent with moving on diversity issues. Connie Jones
might be facing exactly this situation with your Team B. If
Connie's going to be the only one, I think you need to be
especially sensitive to the support she gets from you or
from someone. She's got less experience, and she's a black
female. There are a lot of reasons to say that could be a
very stressful experience. Somehow that needs to be
addressed with others so that she isn't just pushed aside.

The leader, Jan, must hold a goal in this situation to clarify the
practical meaning of TQM vis-à-vis the company's diversity concerns. She can verbally link the new and the old by showing areas
of overlap, complementarity, or if need be, complete rejection of
one set of practices for another. In this example, Jan shows R. J. that
though TQM does not directly address diversity issues, it is quite
consistent with the company's approach to diversity. Jan names two
of Deming's ideas, investing in people and driving out fear, to
demonstrate an overlap with diversity concerns. By doing this, she
has found a way for the existing culture and TQM to coexist.

Be Able to See the Next Steps in Implementing the Ideas

Leaders responsible for implementing new ideas or programs must
step back from the immediate situation and direct attention to
developing understanding of the ideas and their application. They
must help others get past old habits of rote application of techniques or procedures. They must ensure that understanding is sufficient and tools are adequate to allow the ideas to take hold not
simply because they are mandated but because they have their own
value. They must also direct attention to issues and activities that
require further development and effort. Without this, the new
vision or program cannot be thoroughly adopted.

In the following example, Harry, a department manager, ful-
fills this aspect of leadership in a conversation with Helen, who
reports to him.

Harry: The team is getting into the data gathering and TQM
application fairly well. But they don't have anyone in
the leadership role that understands the projects and

help[s] them make the jump from, "Okay, we've got all this data, now how might we go approach that and do something with it?"

Helen: Okay.

Harry: So that, to me, is the challenge.

Notice how Harry communicates his perception of the status of the teams. Notice too how he points to the next step needed in the evolution of the team's ability to use the tools. Effective goal setting keeps the adoption of new ideas on track. Further, Harry's framing of this next step as a challenge (as opposed to a mandate) not only suggests a goal but makes it easier for Helen to enter in if she wants to.

Linking the Needs and the Vision

Consider the five basic needs that we have described.

- Understanding the new ideas
- Seeing how the new ideas are relevant to one's job
- Feeling the enthusiasm of others, especially one's boss, toward the new ideas
- Seeing how the ideas fit with established programs and practices
- Seeing the next steps in implementing the ideas.

For each of these needs, understanding the value of the communicated problem or predicament is one key to effectively communicating a corporate vision or program. Though raising problems can test the assumptions upon which a vision or program is based, it often clarifies the range of choices available and thus points the way to the best fit between the new ideas and the local context. Knowing the true value, then, of communicated problems would, in Senge's terms, show the way for a set of governing ideas to really govern. The question now becomes, What prepares us to handle all of these problem-oriented discussions? As we will see in the remainder of this chapter, the answer lies with our mental models.

Effective Use of Mental Models to Support a Variety of Ends

Mental models tell us how the world works and how we believe it will work in the future. Effective leaders internalize a vision rather than just merely comply with it. To do so, they create a mental model by describing the features or dimensions of the vision that will serve as a basis for judgment. By contrasting the current job situation with the mental model for the vision, they create the frame.

As we saw in Chapter Two, the quality of our framing depends heavily upon the quality of our mental models. In the case of a vision, the quality of our mental models depends upon the thinking that we do around the content, foundation, and associated programs and strategies of the vision.

Vision Content

What do leaders envision? An effective organizational vision may do the following:

- Define a new purpose or mission
- Outline new structures, processes, and systems
- Define the organization's fit with or relationship to its environment

When our vision focuses on mission or purpose, it answers the questions of what the organization is here to do and what the product or service is that should be offered. When our vision focuses on structure, processes, and systems, it defines the kind of organization that is most appropriate for achieving the mission. Such areas of focus describe the necessary structures, information and decision systems, and work processes in both organizational (human) and technical realms. When our vision focuses on environmental relationships, it answers the following questions:

- Who is the customer?
- What is our strategy toward the customer?
- How do we relate to other stakeholders in our community, including suppliers, regulators, and watchdog groups?

The role of mental models in supporting the content of our vision is critical. In most instances, it is not difficult to get employees to see the need to change and to be competitive. Many American workers have mental models for effective competition at the corporate level. Hence, corporate visions at the level of mission or purpose are often readily accepted. Less easily adopted, however, is the vision about how things are done on a daily basis in the engineering division or laboratory or on the factory floor.

The senior management of the organization from which many of the conversations in this book are drawn decided prior to that study, that all traditionally managed plants would convert to self-managing team-based work systems. The company developed an organizational vision that clearly outlined new structures, processes, and systems based on a set of mental models about how high-performance teams function.

However, the mental models that factory employees from traditionally managed systems have in place tell them that they should be cautious about accepting responsibility and that they will not be listened to. Their model for problem resolution is dependent upon the intervention of a higher authority or set of rules; it is not one of problem solving constructively with peers. Leaders trying to present the company vision of the new organization are deluged with reasons why such systems cannot work. Based upon prevailing mental models, these naysayers are right. Leaders at all levels of the company need well-developed mental models of the new structure and processes, especially as they apply to local concerns, or their ability to debate and explain the world in the envisioned future is seriously impaired.

Vision Foundation

The second indicator of the quality of our mental models is clarity about the foundations of our vision. While some visions specifically redefine missions, such as is the case in entrepreneurial organizations that try to soften mission statements to allow their membership more freedom to take advantage of developing opportunities (Bartlett and Ghoshal, 1994), all visions should be based upon a clear purpose or mission and a set of values.

Examine how P. Roy Vagelos, recently retired CEO of Merck,

described the vision from which he operated when he shocked the pharmaceutical industry with Merck's acquisition of the prescription benefits–management company, Medco Containment Services (Nichols, 1994, p. 106).

VISION

MISSION

VALUES

We saw a tremendous opportunity to create a new model for the pharmaceutical industry that would simultaneously improve the quality of health care, help contain costs, and increase Merck's market share. *Expanding our information is critical to achieving these goals:* Medco has data on 38 million patients, which allows us to learn a lot more about how our drugs are prescribed and used, and ultimately, how effective they are in fighting disease. Whether it is cutting-edge scientific information or the reams of data on how doctors prescribe Merck products, *information lies at the heart of what the company does.* Our ability to leverage information will set us apart. Our goal is to maximize the effectiveness of our drugs. *First, we must develop the safest and most effective drugs possible in the labs.* Then, once the drug is on the market and has been prescribed to a patient, *we must be sure that the patient is taking the right drug, that he or she has the appropriate information to take the drug properly, and that the drug will not interfere with other medications the patient is taking.* We can ensure all this by capturing information as it comes through the pharmacy and then putting it into a central data bank that feeds the information back to the physician, the plan sponsor, and ultimately the labs, where it can be used to create new drugs. Medco gives us the ability to link different parts of the health-care-delivery system.

Vagelos' rationale for the acquisition of Medco is a beautiful demonstration of how a future direction is predicated on a crystal clear purpose and a set of values. Vagelos could have presented the vision that guided him by leaving the reference to mission and values implicit rather than explicit. Instead, Vagelos possessed a mental model that was very clear about the interrelationships. Bearing in mind the "reminding" properties of mental models, he went on to frame information as lying "at the heart of what the company does" and to articulate the Merck values of safe and effective drugs. With each explicit framing of mission and values in the context of a specific future direction, each becomes more firmly entrenched in the minds of the organization's members.

Connecting Programs and Strategies

Programs and strategies move an organization toward its vision. With a vision in place, leaders adopt a strategy and a set of programs for driving change. Whether it be zero defects, TQM, High-Commitment Work Systems, team-based management, or right-sizing, we must have a mental model in which the programs and strategies fit the vision.

Shifting patterns in European markets led a client of Bob Sarr's to try to improve profitability in its Western European consumer products business by shifting the focus from traditional large-tonnage low-margin mature (commodity) products to higher-margin lower-tonnage differentiated products. This led to a complementary move to rationalize manufacturing by moving away from individual national control of manufacturing, consolidating production of product lines in one or two locations, eliminating or downsizing sites, and changing work cultures at all remaining sites.

Corporate and manufacturing visions were spelled out and promulgated with varying degrees of clarity. Implementation plans were drawn up, and programs were initiated to support the changes. The manufacturing vision and programs are of particular interest because they exemplify the need for a mental model for a vision and its connecting programs and strategies.

The manufacturing vision called for centers of excellence that were sites dedicated to the production, for all of Europe, of a particular family of products. These sites were to have modern and focused technology, control their own supplier relationships and customer service functions, and be staffed by highly trained employees in self-managing team-based work systems. The vision also spoke of investing in and valuing people.

To drive the change, a number of programs were initiated, including one to improve the thinking capacity of all employees, one designed to support work redesign and reorganization in each site, and corporate-mandated TQM. Simultaneously, central purchasing and distribution functions and other European organizational structures were established. Studies were also initiated to look at manufacturing and distribution costs. Despite all these planned innovations, the traditional business of manufacturing proceeded as it had for decades in most of the eight European locations. Yet, everyone agreed that being more competitive was a good idea and that conditions warranted working on this objective.

When the first of many shutdowns of a manufacturing facility (one product line at a particular site) was announced, people were laid off. The time for framing had come because people had many questions: How does laying people off, no matter how gently or with what benefits, fit in the vision that speaks of valuing and developing people? How does it make any sense to move manufacturing of a product made and sold in Germany to the United Kingdom so the product can be shipped back to Germany? Why should I be willing to learn to redesign my work when the objective is to make me more productive and, if I am more productive, make fewer of us needed? The French know more about products for the French market than do Italians or Danes. Why not manufacture the French goods right here at home?

How do you convince people of the correctness of the center-of-excellence aspect of the manufacturing vision if people think they are already good at making what they make? How do you do it if they do not have a lot of respect for the people in other countries who are about to take their production jobs away? At first glance, shipping things longer distances seems to be a foolish move. Changing the way people relate to the work is also an uphill battle. Why should highly trained specialists learn less demanding skills? Why teach higher skills to those who are content with menial work?

The vision makes sense to people with lots of information and experience because the programs are ways of improving the capacity of the workforce even if they help make the workforce smaller. The vision spells out fewer locations and a smaller workforce as the way to stay in business. Without such a mental model, it will be difficult to help people understand the changes and sacrifices that they are being asked to make.

Moreover, the mental model that connects programs and strategies to the vision must fit the local context. Leaders up and down the line need to paint a picture of local centers of excellence that are greater than the excellence each site has known. They have to paint a picture of life at each site that is more exciting and rewarding than the workforce had thought possible. All the while, they must demonstrate the sense in shipping things across Europe so that manufacturing can be specialized and concentrated and address individuals' concerns—including those of people at risk for unemployment.

The examples in this discussion are intended to point out the critical need to develop our mental models for our vision. The goal, of course, is to frame the content, foundation, and connecting programs and strategies of the vision in ways that are sensible and personally relevant to individual job and unit responsibilities. Only when this is done does the vision have a chance to effect real change. In the next section, we turn to the tools that will develop our mental models for a vision.

Developing Mental Models of the Future: Tools That Leaders Use

Once you understand the importance of mental models, the next step is developing ones that are appropriate for you and for the circumstances in which you find yourself. In this section, we will discuss a number of often used tools—miracle questions, exception framing, and continuous benchmarking—that successful leaders use to bring the vision to life. As we discuss these tools, look for ways to adapt their use to your situation.

Miracle Questions and Exception Framing

In the field of psychology, and particularly in a school of therapy known as brief therapy, *miracle questions* are those that help clients define goals and discover hypothetical solutions to problems (de Shazer, 1988, 1991). Clients might be asked to describe the future as it would look if a particular problem were solved or to tell how a hypothetical videotape of a desired future might look and sound. In asking and eliciting answers to such simple questions, two "miracles" occur. The first is that clients envision the future in some form. The more clients discuss the future, the more they conceive of its existence. Therapists Berg and de Shazer (1993, p. 9) note in this regard, "As client and therapist talk more and more about the solution they want to construct together, they come to believe in the truth or reality of what they are talking about. This is the way that language works, naturally." The second is that clients get in touch with their own expertise for defining solutions to problems (Durrant and Kowalski, 1993).

As an aid to clients who focus on problems rather than the future, therapists ask them to look for exceptions to problem behavior. A client might define a problem in absolute terms ("I can't handle how he always pushes me around"). The therapist will ask the client to frame exceptions to those absolutes ("Was there ever a time you did not let him push you around? What happened?"). Surprisingly, even in the most difficult of circumstances, many clients are able to do this ("Well, there was the time . . ."). By framing exceptions, client and therapist slowly begin to unfreeze realities that look so hard and fast. Then, by asking future-oriented questions, new realities begin to look more possible.

Phrased properly, questions about the future are miracle questions. They are not about prediction but about forming a picture of what might be if we got what we want. They are powerful tools for leaders who are headed into uncertain environments and must develop visions for corporations or for units of such corporations.

Why do miracle questions work? They release us from the present and all the intractable problems that go with it. They help us clarify our goals and desires for the future, and they expand our ideas about what might be possible. By framing exceptions, such as finding examples of those "lazy" factory workers being quite ambitious, we also expand our ideas about what is possible. We remove a fixed mental model ("always lazy") with one that is more accurate and offers more possibilities ("sometimes lazy, sometimes ambitious").

Corporate reengineers use miracle questions when they ask, for example: "If you could start from scratch, what would this company look like? How would you run this place?" The hallmark of reengineering efforts is that once the vision is secured, everything else is cast aside. This feature of reengineering prompted Michael Hammer, coauthor of *Reengineering the Corporation,* to state, "To succeed at reengineering, you have to be a visionary, a motivator, and a leg breaker" (Stewart, 1993).

But the miracle question is also surfacing in the advice that consultants are bringing to bear on any change effort. Examine what Boston Consulting Group vice president Jeanie Daniel Duck said in a 1993 *Harvard Business Review* article on managing change.

> Top management should start by requiring a change of behavior, and when that yields improved performance, the excitement and belief will follow. The first change in behavior should be that of the top executives. Leaders need to ask themselves, "If we were managing the way we say we want to manage, how would we act? How would we attack our problems? What kind of meetings and conversations would we have? Who would be involved? How would we define, recognize, compensate, and reward appropriate behavior?" As leaders and followers work side by side to develop the answers to these questions, they create their futures together [p. 112].

Duck poses several miracle questions that could lead to changes in reward systems, management styles, dealings with stakeholders, communications, and approaches to decision making. Duck's quote is clearly directed to top management, and, indeed, most reengineers are either outsiders or senior managers. Yet, as we will see, the miracle question and exception framing can most emphatically apply to everyday leaders.

First, let's acknowledge that new corporate visions or programs of any kind can be an alien presence that provokes fear, intimidation, and/or confusion. (Surely TQM's statistical process control features engendered fear in those less mathematically inclined.) Second, the people affected most by the new changes sometimes feel pressure to adopt the vision or program whole cloth instead of asking "What do I need?" or "What is useful for me?" But adoption of a vision or new program has to be incremental, problem by problem, situation by situation (Bennis, 1993). The beauty of the miracle question is that it enables potential users of a vision or program to define their own use. It helps them consider the vision's implications for their circumstances.

Let's return to Bob and Fred's conversation, presented earlier in the chapter, about the charting tools associated with TQM. See if you can determine why this conversation is greatly in need of a miracle question.

Bob: He sent me this chart, okay?
Fred: I'll never understand all these charts.
Bob: [*Laughs.*] That one where they did the fishbone exercise gave me heartburn. I told Mark, our trainer, it gave me heartburn. I'm not sure he appreciated it.

On the surface, this conversation looks innocuous. Some might even call it small talk. But what is the effect? Fred expressed a problem with the charting aspects of TQM that he framed in absolute terms ("I'll never understand all these charts"). Bob's "heartburn" response clearly reinforced Fred's feelings of frustration. Bob failed to understand that, as the leader of the plant, his example with respect to TQM was critical. Bob missed an opportunity to explore how Fred might use TQM and its tools. He could have done so with a future-oriented question such as, "Can you imagine any circumstance in which you might be able to use the data from such a tool?" He could also have tried some exception framing with, "Has there ever been a time you used a charting method and it helped?"

The death knell sounds gradually in the failure to implement an organizational vision or new program. It occurs in the accumulation of all those seemingly inconsequential conversations when the possible futures offered by a vision or program get overlooked. Had the plant manager used the miracle question, even if he himself did not know what the answer to the question might be, Fred might have surprised both of them with his answer. But Fred was never given the opportunity to think aloud about the implications of the charting tools for his situation and so begin to develop a mental model for the charting methods. This seemingly inconsequential conversation is typical of the many thousands of day-to-day conversations that maim or kill many a well-designed and expensive corporate vision or program.

Continuous Benchmarking: Getting to Points B and A

Much as the lessons of miracle questions and exception framing must be seen as critical to developing our mental models, it is important to recognize that the development of mental models is a continuous process. We must continuously analyze our vision, its programs and strategies, and the local contexts in which we operate. This is the key to developing our mental models and addressing the inevitable problems that surface. Ralph Stayer (1990), CEO of Johnsonville Foods, Inc., of Sheboygan, Wisconsin, calls this process "Getting to Points B and A."

In the *Harvard Business Review,* Stayer wrote eloquently about his journey in pursuing an organizational vision for Johnsonville Sausage, a successful family-owned business that required radical change. Point B was determined by posing the miracle question and picturing the end state, the image of what an ideal sausage company would look like: "The image that best captured the organizational end state I had in mind for Johnsonville was a flock of geese on the wing. I didn't want an organizational chart with traditional lines and boxes, but a 'V' of individuals who knew the common goal, took turns leading, and adjusted their structure to the task at hand. Geese fly in a wedge, for instance, but land in waves. Most important, each individual bird is responsible for its own performance" (p. 67).

Point A was Stayer's authoritarian management style and set of business practices that kept others in his company from becoming self-leading. While this propelled a number of actions, the fascinating aspect of Stayer's journey is that Points B and A were continually reformulated. As he took actions to get from Point A to Point B, he found that B changed, and as B changed, A would change as well. For example, authoritarian control led to delegation to three top managers. But this proved unsuccessful because the managers were incapable of making independent decisions. In firing these managers, Stayer learned he could not give responsibility; instead, "people had to expect it, want it, and even demand it" (1990, p. 72). So he wound up revising Point B by deciding that he needed to become a better coach and communicate a vision. That led to some new Point A behaviors such as encouraging plants to solve their own problems and turn them into opportuni-

ties. By taking successive measures, he developed new benchmarks
of where he was and where he wanted to be, all the while developing his mental models for each.

Framing the Past, Present, and Future

To this point, we have spoken only in generalities about the need
for continuous benchmarking of the present state, A, and the
vision-based end state, B. From a communications perspective, we
have to frame from both points. Often it is useful to frame how
things are (Point A) in ways that help others understand and
hence more easily change present beliefs. Moving forward requires
framing Point B. It is useful as we develop our skill at framing to
understand and be conscious of two modes of reasoning com-
monly used to help us frame: case-based and rule-based reasoning.

Case-Based Reasoning and the Framing of Experience

Think of your mental models as coming from a library of "cases,"
or stories. In each case, there is a problem or an event of importance. Also in each case, there is a solution and lesson to be
learned, which is the point of the case.

A good demonstration of the usefulness of this library of cases
comes from the work of scientists who study human reasoning
processes. These cognitive scientists study how we reason, draw
inferences, and explain the world to others. For a long time they
thought that when we became experts on a subject, we reasoned
by using a set of rules (Schank, 1986; Kolodner and Riesbeck, 1986;
Riesbeck and Schank, 1989). Their most current work suggests,
however, that we reason less from a set of rules and more from
prior cases that serve as reminders.

Christopher Riesbeck and Roger Schank (1989) use a baseball
example to demonstrate this idea. Which second baseman should
the manager of the Mets play regularly in the upcoming World
Series—the rookie sensation, the steady hustler who helped with the
World Series the previous year, or the guy who did the best this year?
While we can cite a rule, "Experience is the most important factor
in a pennant race," the answer is not so clear cut. They write, "But
even though we can cite rules like these, actual decision making in

such cases is usually more seat-of-the-pants in nature. We have a gut feeling about the situation as a whole" (p. 10).

We use a certain reasoning at the time a decision is made because we are reminded of a prior case based upon the one that we are currently confronting. Riesbeck and Schank call this case-based reasoning, because the current situation causes us to retrieve a prior case from memory, determine its relevance, and decide what to do based upon what happened in that prior case.

Don and Sally's conversation (in Chapter Two) provides a perfect example of case-based reasoning. As you may recall, Don, the team leader, was explaining to Sally why the team needed more time to struggle with making its own decisions. Note what Don said about crisis situations: "The way I tend to operate is, if we are in some crisis mode, *as was often the case in my last job,* then I am prescriptive if necessary. I would say frequently, 'Here's what we have to do.' My sense is that we're not in a crisis mode, so we have ample time and opportunity for . . . participation" [emphasis added].

Don found himself in a new situation. His current job reminded him that his old job was very different and so helped him to respond differently. Certainly a rule could be abstracted from Don's thinking, such as, "In crisis situations, be prescriptive; in non-crisis situations, be participative," but Don reasons and explains the world more from his experience than from a rule.

There is nothing wrong with rules; certainly we hold many of them. But for every rule, there are often countless exceptions. When situations get complex, even experts in a given area frequently cite previous cases with which they have been involved that remind them of the current case. It is for exactly this reason, Riesbeck and Schank note (1989, pp. 6–7), that case-based reasoning is taught in schools of law and business: "Why do law schools and business schools teach cases? It seems obvious that both of these subjects are inherently case-based. . . . It seems obvious that knowing the law in the sense of being able to practice law effectively means knowing the cases or at least knowing where to find the cases when you need them. Thus, for law at least, knowledge means knowledge of cases."

Riesbeck and Schank go on to say that the use of cases in business is slightly different.

There are some principles of business that you can learn in business school. But, to make money, which is the intent of business after all, you cannot simply follow the successful cases of the past. You have to reason from a prior case by attempting to understand what principles they teach, apart from the particulars of the given context in which this case occurred. After all, if there were simply one successful paradigmatic case to be followed, everyone would follow it and every businessman would be rich. In business, each new case changes the world sufficiently so that the methods that were specifically applied may not work again. Those methods might work, however, in a different industry, or with a different product, or in a different city. A very standard way of conducting business then, is to replicate what others have done, but not to do it identically.

What Riesbeck, Schank, and other cognitive scientists teach is that law and business are not the oddballs of education or of reasoning. We reason from experience—from prior cases—and we make new decisions by abstracting the essentials from an appropriate prior case. This, too, is how we frame. The case from which we reason leads to the framing of our experience, precisely as we saw in the conversation between Don and Sally.

If our present-based Point A mental models develop case by case, how do we develop mental models for Point B, our vision? The same way—we envision or create future scenarios, and these scenarios provide us with cases. We can look at future meetings, production dilemmas, economic situations, or battle scenarios. By making the effort to anticipate likely future scenarios right down to typical conversations, we can develop highly functional mental models for our vision-based Point B. From the naval battles enacted by Admiral Nelson to the computer models used by Peter Senge, Point B has been created in mental space and used for framing.

Rule-Based Reasoning and the Framing of Principles

Principles and rules are another part of the models that we build. Principles are usually standards to which we expect others or ourselves to adhere as a rule. Rules are usually based on cases from the past, but they have come to be simple givens that we accept as true or right. Some rules are quite useful and serve us well. Others may have lost their validity and get in our way. A critical examination of the rules that make up our mental models is certainly useful from time to time, so that we may examine the validity of our assumptions (Senge, 1990).

In addition, we must be ready to help others who do not accept our rules to see the value in them. When this need arises, we may resort to cases (stories) as a method of demonstrating the validity or usefulness of a rule. In the field of organizational development, for example, there is a widely accepted rule that effective team size for a true high-performance team cannot exceed twelve members. Yet that rule is widely resisted. Often it is necessary to illustrate with cases of large ineffective teams to help others understand the validity of the rule. That is why framing based on cases is so powerful. It helps us to remember why a rule exists in the first place.

Just as case-based reasoning leads to the framing of experience, rule-based reasoning leads to the framing of rules or principles. In the case of an organizational vision, the framing of our principles usually takes place in the context of some overall philosophy or framework of related ideas. Within this framework, we mark the interrelationship between the ideas through our language.

Philosopher Kenneth Burke (1954, 1957, 1962) has suggested that people infuse certain ideas with great positive value or meaning, which he calls "god" terms. People infuse other ideas with a negative or low value, which he calls "devil" terms.

Strong framing is driven by the fact that there is a clear idea of what is good and a clear idea of why sacrifice or extra effort may be required. By paying attention to and using "god" and "devil" terms, we can improve our capacity to frame our vision. Some of the success of the Total Quality movement, for example, is certainly due to the choice of quality as a "god" term. *Quality* identifies a key principle with which nearly all can agree. As a result, the quality concept has the capacity to transcend disagreements among people with conflicting interests, even managers reluctant to share power and employees reluctant to exert maximum effort. Read Deming's vision of quality, and you get a sense of its importance.

> I want to make it clear that as you improve quality, your costs go down. That is one of the main lessons that the Japanese learned and that American management . . . couldn't care less about.

Interested in finance, creative accounting. That's all right. But when it means that you ignore the fundamentals of improvement, it is not right. Improve quality. Your costs go down. Fewer mistakes, fewer breakdowns. . . . To zero? No. But more and more. Continual reduction in mistakes, continual improvement of quality, mean lower and lower costs [Walton, 1986, p. 26].

The "god" term is not labeled as such, but Deming's language makes it apparent how central and important the concept of quality is. It is associated with the success of the Japanese, the ignorance of American management, the most direct and fundamental way to lower costs, and, by implication, the means to succeed in business.

A "devil" term, as you might expect, is just the opposite of a "god" term. Like "god" terms, a "devil" term is not identified as such for others. It is a concept infused with negative value that clearly identifies that which is evil and to be avoided. One of Burke's many insights is that the avoidance of some evil is a frequent motivation for change. Hence, "devil" terms are the impetus for many a vision. For example, a "devil" term for many corporations in the forties and fifties was *union*. It drove many leaders to envision union-free environments invested with many positive attributes.

Examine what Deming had to say about fear: "What are people afraid of? Afraid to contribute to the company. Better not get out of line. Don't violate procedures. Do it exactly this way. . . . Fear takes a horrible toll. Fear is all around, robbing people of their pride, hurting them, robbing them of a chance to contribute to the company. It is unbelievable what happens when you unloose fear" (Walton, 1986, p. 73).

We can see how Deming used fear as a "devil" term. He associated it with words like "horrible," "robbing," and "hurting." Clearly, conditions that create fear in organizations should be avoided at all cost.

There is a third type of term that Burke calls "good" terms. Usually a vision is accompanied by a subordinate set of terms that are positive and in some way related to the central concept or "god" term. "Good" terms don't have the ultimate power of the "god" term, but they still have a very high value. Thus, by virtue of their relationship to the "god" term, "good" terms form a hierarchy of beliefs. Consider TQM's "good" terms of *right the first time, just-in-time, customer needs, continuous improvement,* and *teamwork,* to name just a few. Strong framing is helped by the fact that these terms are clearly linked to the "god" term quality. There is a clear understanding of "what goes with what" that can be applied to the complex environment for which change is sought.

In the following dialogue, Art, a manufacturing manager, communicates his TQM expectations to Carl, who is in charge of running one of the unit's manufacturing lines. This line is run by a group of technicians who produce labels for one of the company's products. Pay particular attention to Art's language.

> *Art:* You should know that I expect you to be out there monitoring what is going on and helping to troubleshoot the problem. Just make sure that we recognize the effort that went into getting the labels right the first time.
> *Carl:* [*Laughs.*]
> *Art:* Certainly, that is what I consider a Total Quality approach to this project.

In this brief conversation, Art is framing the TQM vision in more concrete terms for Carl by singling out the behaviors that meet his expectations for quality, the "god" term. Note also Art's use of *right the first time,* which is a TQM "good" term that tells workers to put the effort into quality from the beginning. Carl found this humorous because, as other dialogue revealed, this work unit was not known for getting it right the first time. Finally, note Art's use of the terms *monitoring* and *troubleshoot,* which are also related to other TQM "good" terms such as continuous improvement, which requires workers constantly to be on the alert for ways to improve the process. Art applied his mental model for quality to Carl's management responsibilities and framed those behaviors that were consistent with his mental model.

There is great variety in the number of terms that a vision statement might have. Not all need the number of terms that TQM has. We also found that "god" and "devil" terms can sometimes vary by subculture or individual unit within the same organization. One interesting example of this occurred in a university department that had divided itself in two camps. Even though the university's mission was both research and teaching, each camp perceived encroachment by the other on the department's resources. To the teachers, *teaching* became a "god" term and *research* became a "devil" term. To the researchers, research became a "god" term and teaching became a "devil" term. These terms emerged not because teachers resented research or researchers resented teaching per se. They emerged because teachers and researchers resented each other. The chairman of the department had to find another "god" term that would transcend and unite both camps. He did this by speaking repeatedly of a *diversified mission*. A "good" term he associated with his "god" term was the *need to do all things well*. Each time members of either camp began to use their respective "god" and "devil" terms, the department chair's task was to reframe the situation using his "god" term, diversified mission. Note that this was possible because the department chair had first constructed a mental model for his specific department, not just the organization as a whole.

If you can cast your mental models for your vision with a set of "god" and "devil" terms, you will have very clearly brought these models to the surface by identifying their attributes and the relationships among them. As such, they will serve as a strong benchmark against which current circumstances can be measured and clearly communicated.

Read what Tom Nies, CEO of Cincom Systems, one of the world's largest privately held computer-software companies, said in relaying his vision (Modic, 1989): "Whom the gods would destroy they first make arrogant. . . . Therefore, the proper attitude for accelerating and aiding growth seems to be humility. Remembering and realizing that our knowledge is limited but our ignorance is immeasurable, humility is the only possible correct attitude for the knowledgeable person. Only the ignorant can rationalize prideful and arrogant behavior or thinking. Because of this, it is not only old dogs who cannot learn new tricks, but even more so our own prideful selves" (p. 23).

Can you identify the "god" and "devil" terms that Nies used? Read on to see what he said about leadership: "A large number of CEOs behave in an aloof manner (but) demonstrate that their heart is not in the business. (A CEO who limits his exposure creates a feeling that) he is better than the other people. That leads to an atmosphere of arrogance that sets a model for others to behave in the same way. . . . The senior executive officer of an organization must be the servant of those who are serving his clients and his other people" (p. 23).

The "devil" terms that pop out to us immediately are *pride* and *arrogance*. They are frequently contrasted with the "god" terms of *humility* and *servitude* in Nies's view of leaders as servants. What is especially noteworthy about this vision is the way in which the role of the CEO as servant follows directly from the vision's principles. Cincom has been described as a company with a vision, and it is clear to see why Tom Nies is the man behind it.

We can see in these examples that "god" and "devil" terms are defined through contrasting a clear good and a clear evil. A hierarchy of beliefs gets established when other subordinate "good" terms get associated with the "god" term. Do you have "god" and "devil" terms in your mental models? Take a moment to identify them for yourself and to be sure they are effective.

A Backward Glance at This Chapter

Warren Bennis wrote in *An Invented Life* (1993) that the field of leadership needs more good stories. This recommendation makes even more sense in light of the importance of framing our past, present, and future. In discussing the importance of visions and frames, we made the following points in this chapter:

- Visions are the foundation of leadership.
- Many people, managers and leaders alike, need to learn how to perform the framing necessary to realize the visions.
- Leaders must frame the vision in order to help organizational members make sense of the vision, see its relevance to their responsibilities, feel others' enthusiasm for it, see the fit to established programs and practices, and see the next steps in implementing the vision.
- To meet all of the organization's communication needs, leaders must develop their mental models for a vision based on its content, foundation, and connecting programs and strategies.
- Three tools—miracle questions, exception framing, and continuous benchmarking—can be especially helpful in developing our mental models.

- Miracle questions help us to envision a future and clarify our goals.
- If we can frame exceptions to problem behavior, we can also remove obstacles to achieving the goal.
- Continuous benchmarking allows the development of our mental models by taking successive measurements of where we are (Point A) and where we want to be (Point B).
- The framing that occurs as we contrast current circumstances with the vision will be case based, rule based, or a combination of the two.
- Case-based reasoning leads us to the framing of experience.
- Rules-based reasoning leads to the framing of our principles. When this is done well, "god" and "devil" terms are often used in the framing.

In this chapter, we have made much of the need to fit the vision to the local context. In Chapter Four, we examine the role of context in detail.

Chapter Four

Context Sensitivity
Recognizing Opportunities and Constraints

As we saw in Chapter Three, Ralph Stayer understood that in order for his vision of a self-managing organization to be fully realized at Johnsonville Foods, it would have to be continuously reformulated. He knew that successive steps toward (and sometimes away from) the vision would be necessary. He also came to realize that he didn't directly control the performance of his people, but that they essentially managed themselves. Stayer felt that his primary role was to manage the context through the allocation of resources and the availability of various systems and structures. This led him to redesign the quality control system and institute teams.

Stayer's insight about managing the context is particularly useful. He recognized that in any given conversation between two or more people in his company, the context is defined by those elements that shape the way people think and what they expect. Usually those elements include the people present, the locale or setting, the activities, a global sense of the encounter as it is unfolding, and the background knowledge that goes with each element. These components are arranged in such a way that they take on a gestalt quality, where the various parts are seen as a unified whole (which leads us to refer to *the* context). Because of this gestalt quality, if one of the components changes, we consider the context to have changed.

An ability to read the context directly affects framing effectiveness. Organizational scientist Gareth Morgan (1986) writes that effective leaders seem to have a deep appreciation of context; for them, the process of reading context occurs at an almost subconscious level.

Those who believe that effective leaders are born and not made may take this as discouraging news. We believe, however, that the ability to read context can be learned and cultivated. People can learn to read those all important opportunities to break into the action and influence its course. People can also learn to recognize the constraints that limit or restrict their movement into the flow of communications. In this chapter, we focus on the role that context plays in framing and the ways you can become more sensitive to opportunities and constraints.

Context Insensitivity: A Destructive Trap

Just as we sometimes drive to a destination without consciously considering the route, many of us move through our everyday encounters unaware of the opportunities for framing. We take a familiar context for granted and implicitly buy into the myth that by talking we communicate. But if talk by itself guaranteed communication, there would never be any communication breakdowns—and the reality is that the world is filled with them.

But learning about context is no guarantee of heeding its opportunities and constraints. That fact was brought home to us when we visited a factory to promote a training exercise that paired leaders and unit members together in two-way expectation sharing and renegotiation of their relationship. We called the training "interpersonal contracting," because an informal or implied contract was the intended outcome. Unfortunately, not until after our arrival did we learn that the factory had recently fought an attempted unionization of the workforce, and antiunion sentiment was still running very high. So when the factory's leadership saw words such as "contract" and "renegotiate" in our materials, we unwittingly struck a raw nerve. The words we used evoked everything that they negatively associated with union-management relations. It wasn't long before we were on an airplane out of town, having learned to pay more attention to context, both in advance and on the spot.

We made the mistake of viewing the plant as just one of many similar manufacturing plants in a large organization. But the context—the recent and hard-won campaign to prevent unionization at the factory—made the plant special and made management extremely sensitive to the issues evoked by our language. This difference from other plants made the gestalt different, and our communications were ineffective as a result. Had we framed the exercise in other terms, we might have had a chance of running an effective program.

Navigating the Context Successfully

One of the lessons of the experience just described is that as leaders, we must learn to interpret and evaluate the opportunities and possibilities for our framing attempts. Through context sensitivity, we learn the who, what, where, when, why, and how of framing effectiveness. To develop this sensitivity, we can ask the following questions:

- Who is involved?
- What is this person's interest?
- What are the possibilities for action?
- What are my limitations?
- Where are there gaps in understanding?
- When can I best intervene?
- Why are people responding as they are?
- Why is a new frame needed here?
- How can I establish a new frame?

By regularly asking these questions and others like them, we can gather the knowledge of context necessary to adapt ourselves to the uniqueness of each situation that we face. In the following sections, we explore the key arenas for improving our awareness of context, from knowing the overall culture to defining our own principles.

Raising the Periscope: Know the Culture, Business Environment, and Surrounding Events

We often see our framing attempts as a function of someone else's previous communication. This is demonstrated nicely when we observe people in the midst of a conflict: one response triggers another, tensions escalate, and tempers flare. The immediate context for a framing attempt is often the previous framing attempt of another. The immediate context also contains a set of variables, such as a new person entering the conversation or a change in topic.

By raising a periscope to see the overall picture, we enable ourselves to see the broader influences on context. These influences are relatively enduring because they come from our societal and organizational culture or from a particular business and economic environment.

On the subject of culture, Edgar Schein (1985) argued that patterns of culture form around assumptions we make about human nature, work, freedom, reality, and human relationships. Schein says that while we are likely aware of our values that spring from these beliefs, the beliefs themselves are held in our unconscious and surface only when there has been a cultural rule violation.

The following example demonstrates a cultural rule violation and how culture influences our framing. The manager, Bill, is giving one of his female team leaders, Alice, some positive feedback:

Bill: I think you handled the meeting very well. I think that it was kept from being very political.
Alice: Yes.
Bill: And it could have been. It could have turned out to be a real pissing contest between Tom and Chuck.
Alice: Mm-hmm.

No matter what his intent, Bill's frame of the potential conflict between Tom and Chuck as a pissing contest is culturally inappropriate in this context for two reasons. First, crude language is considered inappropriate for most business settings. Second, the masculine reference to a pissing contest privileges a male perspective, and since the person to whom Bill is speaking is female, the inappropriateness of his reference is magnified.

Like Bill, though, we all occasionally violate cultural rules. We know the rules even though we may not think or talk of them. We know about crude language, and we know that racist or sexist language is culturally or interpersonally inappropriate in organizations. Other cultural norms are also important, to varying degrees in different cultures. Every culture has a few norms that are of special note and that we do well to observe.

Deference to those higher in the power structure is a norm that people often associate with Eastern cultures, but it appears to be a strong norm in the United States and Europe as well. Indeed, in most organizations, one is more polite and more careful when addressing those in higher positions and more gentle and circumspect in giving unpleasant feedback.

Thoroughness is a norm in some corporate cultures and not in others. In large and stable organizations, there is often time to check and recheck positions, and the cost of errors outweighs the cost of delay. In fast-moving situations, however, the cost of thoroughness is too high in light of the need for rapid decisions and action. Such cultures build in an expectation for occasional failure due to an inability to cover all the bases. A related point is that, speed, a norm often in direct conflict with thoroughness, is characteristic of organizations in rapidly developing markets. Those who cannot grasp quickly or decide quickly or who require too much background and supporting data are not likely to succeed in such cultures.

Most organizations have norms about taking risks. In some, the taking of a risk that has been carefully studied and understood is rewarded and culturally valued. In others, the cultural norm is to take no risk; there, inaction may meet with greater cultural approval than even slightly risky behaviors. However, newcomers to an organization must recognize that a concern for thoroughness does not necessarily mean risk taking is not valued.

Some organizations have developed a culture of valuing. All employees are respected as individuals, and their thoughts and ideas are deemed worthy of attention and response. Individuals are noticed or recognized by corporate rituals, and managers are expected to do things to promote valuing. In other, often fast-moving settings, individuals come and go and are seen more in terms of their role and function. In such organizations, valuing is not likely to be a cultural norm.

Appearances of a certain sort can be part of a cultural norm. Appearing cool under fire, self-assured, in charge, or leaderlike may be a norm; less likely, but also possible, is a norm that requires that one appear sensitive and warm. The latter norm might hold in a social services organization or in the human resources section of a larger organization. Appearance norms also extend to physical appearance and manners of dress. The standard uniform of three-piece suit and wingtip shoes is an example of one norm that is difficult for women to meet culturally.

The norm that says members must conform can go well beyond dress codes. One of the powerful features of cultural norms is that they are not explicit. Their inexplicitness or fuzziness makes them hard to confirm and hard to fight. In certain organizations, there are strong implicit codes about what to cultivate and what to avoid in social causes, political parties, places to live, and schools for one's children. In addition, it is implicitly advisable to keep regular sorts of hours and to not adopt personal habits outside of a certain band. Conformity is not overtly required or demanded, but the cultural norm of conformity allows the organization to make detrimental judgments about those who do not "fit in" when it comes time to promote or reward.

Any framing opportunity will be shaped by one or more of the factors just named. For example, several European subsidiaries of Colgate-Palmolive recently encountered a conflict between the demands of the business environment and their organizational culture. Both the general business environment in Europe and the organization's hierarchy were quite supportive of greater self-management and shop floor team structures. However, the history and culture of the various European subsidiaries clearly supported deference to the hierarchy, extreme risk avoidance, and a focus on appearances. These cultural factors made it extremely difficult for the subsidiaries' management to create an upward flow of communications within their own organization and to initiate the upward communication of difficult issues beyond their subsidiary. Even if the subsidiaries wanted to do it, challenging top management about some top-down practices that interfered with local risk taking and autonomy seemed nearly impossible. Taking the risks necessary to change to a self-managing culture at the factory level was made terribly stressful by the need to avoid risk and maintain appearances.

In an organizational setting that avoids risk, it is critical to frame even slightly risky behaviors or proposals more carefully than in a setting with a high tolerance for risk. It may be better to minimize or quantify the actual risk, stress potential gains, or stress the risk of not trying the proposed behavior.

In a culture that demands deference to authority, subordinates may have more difficulty in framing; in many ways, they are forced to sacrifice their right to frame. Proposals that are significant departures from what has gone before might be seen as insufficiently deferential to those higher in the hierarchy who may have originated those early ideas. To frame a new method as a "correction of past mistakes" is not very deferential. Better to frame the new method as an "improvement upon past practices." Because of the expected deference to the ideas of the manager, subordinate members may also be polite, even enthusiastic, about ideas or proposals that do not appeal to them. Thus, the manager gets either little feedback or feedback that is diluted with disclaimers or inflated with superlatives. Framing in a deferential culture places a disproportionately heavy emphasis on relationship goals and requires people to juggle multiple goals, as described in Chapter Two. Culture's influence on framing may be less visible than the demands of task goals, but it is no less profound. In many ways, cultural rules are the social glue of the situations in which we operate.

We must also be careful to acknowledge the influence of the general business environment in which we operate. What is the economy doing? What are the general trends and forecasts for projected resources and budgets? What are the new technologies? What new business trends have emerged in our organization, profession, industry, or field? Knowledge of our resource base and general trends in the environment influence how we frame as we explain and justify our vision, the utilization of resources, new or existing policies, or other proposed change efforts.

Ralph Stayer found this out when people on the shop floor complained about others whose performance was marginal. They demanded that senior management "either fix them or fire them." Stayer said his first reaction was to respond to the immediacy of the complaint. But a quick recheck of his self-managing vision made him realize that the people on the shop floor had the resources to best deal with shop floor performance issues. So Stayer advised them that senior management could offer help in setting performance standards and coaching poor performers, but that would be all; those on the shop floor had to own and deal with the problem. To Stayer's surprise, the plant members actually fired the individuals who failed to meet team standards. This check on existing resources in Johnsonville's internal business environment also proved quite valuable in shaping its new human resources system.

Clearly, we need to be very aware of the cultural and business settings in which we work. We cannot formulate or adopt a vision, much less advocate for it, unless we understand our cultural and business environment. To keep abreast of the general business environment, we need to attend to current trends and forecasts at local, national, and international levels. Professional and industry meetings, literature in the field, and networking can all be useful, as can an occasional time-out just to ponder what it all means.

A good way to know our cultural environments is to pay attention to everyday cultural rule violations. Observe the consequences of a violation and note how the cultural rule is supplied in the process. In effect, try to become a stranger in your own land as much as possible, so you can remain fresh and new to the distinguishing features of your culture.

Examining the Frame: Know the Audience's Beliefs and How They Might Be Changed

Simply put, if we become sensitive to the mental models of others and the specific frames those models may produce, we can read framing opportunities and constraints more clearly. We can then adapt our message. If we communicate that we understand another's perspective, we show regard because we have taken the time to consider an alternative view. If we show genuine regard, people tend to be more favorably disposed toward us. As one step in this process of developing sensitivity to the frames of those with whom you communicate, ask yourself the following questions:

- What frames are the people in my audience likely to hold based on their experience or training?
- Are their frames permeable?
- Where is the audience's space for new thinking?

Which Frame Is in Place?

Consider the feedback a team member, Hank, gives to his team leader, Marty. Examine how Hank takes Marty's perspective into account in relaying the feedback:

Hank: I think you and I are on the same page a lot of times. You feel like you are up against the wall. You're fighting a lot of battles these days over things you feel strongly about and things you think are right to do. But I think you need to go further and break down the barriers, especially on the staffing problem.

Marty: Break down the barriers, okay.

Hank: Break them right down. Show your leadership and say, "Hey, time for discussion is over. Your decision is going to end up costing the company money. We can't do it, and this is the way it is." Show the unit that you're leading now. Show them that you are a leader among leaders.

Hank's "breaking down the barriers" frame is much more effective because of the time he takes to acknowledge Marty's position. Marty may not necessarily believe that he should adopt the stance that Hank is advocating, but Hank's efforts at least guarantee an audience more willing to listen to his message.

Sometimes, however, the problem is that we are all too familiar with others' frames, because they are held so firmly that they cannot see past them. We say to ourselves, "What will it take to get this person to change?"

How Permeable Is the Frame?

In addition to trying to assess what frames a person or group holds, we frequently have to assess up front how permeable those frames are. A permeable frame is not one that is necessarily ill formed, weakly held, or tenuous in any way—only one that has a capacity to embrace new elements (Kelly, 1955). Thus, reframing is possible to the degree the other's frames are permeable and let in new information.

Introducing new elements into a person's frame and therefore helping to develop his or her mental models can cause the frame to change a lot or just a little. More often than not, we can help others expand their frames if we take the time to become more sensitive to their mental models.

This was highlighted for the authors recently when a bank branch manager shared a story about her older customers. She told us that potential customers who have been around since the Depression and witnessed the collapse of several savings and loan institutions often have very firmly held mental models regarding banks, which include the beliefs that banks are not stable and should not be trusted. Our bank manager also discovered that older customers' frames of her bank are permeable. For them, she frames the bank as a "longtime member of the community" or as "established in 1904"; she deliberately avoids the frames of "young and aggressive staff" and "desire for increased market share," which are more appealing to younger customers.

But how can we know what the best frame is? We can learn about others' mental models by posing a few well-placed questions about their interests, needs, desires, opinions, blind-spots, and pet peeves. We can get some sense of what makes others tick. If we know how to get their attention, we can adjust our framing accordingly. We can find their space for new thinking.

Where Can New Thinking Enter In?

Another way to permeate others' frames is to discover how the present frame fails to take into account some important aspect of the current context. Organizations in the midst of a change effort, for example, negatively frame the company's competitive situation, market position, technological base, or overall financial performance and create a sense of urgency about the need to take action (Kotter, 1995). Management focuses "on the potential revenue drop when an important patent expires, the five-year trend in declining core businesses, or an emerging market that everyone seems to be ignoring" (p. 60). By showing why the status quo is unacceptable, change agents hope to create feelings of discomfort around existing ways of thinking and thus lay the necessary foundation for an acceptance of change and a new vision. Without the framing of an urgent need, people will not be driven out of their comfort zones.

For example, an old freight railroader interprets most events in the context of a world in which freight is key. Those in a tourist railroad see the passenger as king or queen. New thinking for the person at each extreme comes when each is helped to see how today's mixed railroad environment is both similar to and different from either of the two extreme railroad models. Again, if we can show them how their frames are lacking in some way, their frames become more permeable.

Many an authoritarian manager has framed the move to team-based systems as abandoning "a command and control structure" to move to a "chaotic, loose group of workers with lots of warm-fuzzy–type interactions." However, the way to permeate the old frame is not to expound on all of the nice warm-fuzzy features of teams. Rather, it is to carefully and thoroughly show how command and control is provided for in new ways that are understandable to a person in the old command-and-control frame. For example, we might show how information that was provided within a command structure will still be provided but at different points and with different responses by those in team structures. In this situation, as in any other, knowing the frame and the mental model that supports it is critical to learning how to bring about change through reframing.

Using the Internal Compass of Your Principles

How much do we look to others or to immediate circumstances to guide our choices? Do we ask, "What would my boss want me to do? What will my peers think? What would the old-timer do in this circumstance?" If we are inclined to look outward rather than inward for the criteria by which we choose our actions, we may find ourselves on unsteady ground.

For any given framing opportunity, if we rely primarily on the immediate context rather than our vision and values, little harm may be done. However, unless we make use of the internal compass that vision and values provide, we are likely to be inconsistent in our response to situations, similar though they may be. Over time and across the various contexts in which we participate, we may find that (perhaps quite unintentionally) we flip-flop.

Consistency needs to be an element in our adaptation to current circumstances. Introducing consistency in our response does not mean that we are less adaptive to a situation. Rather, we are adaptive in ways that are consistent with one another across similar sets of circumstances. Consistency is not so much valued for the predictability it affords but for the criteria guiding our choices. It reflects our principles. For example, we cannot successfully frame safety as a "paramount objective" in one circumstance while paying it scant heed in another. If we do, others trying to gauge our mind-set usually come up confused.

Jim is a professional who is easily influenced. He is not young and therefore impressionable; he is impressionable because he consistently looks to others in the immediate context to define the situation. When his communication partners change, so do "the facts" of a situation and his response to it. Sometimes it seems he will say almost anything. People who communicate with Jim come away asking, "What does he stand for? What are his principles?"

One could argue that Jim is highly sensitive to context and merely adapting himself to each situation. But when similar contexts produce divergent responses, we are likely to attribute to Jim qualities such as wishy-washy, unstable, or unprincipled. We see flip-flops. Jim has little conscious knowledge of his own principles and hence has difficulty drawing from them. This produces weak mental models and causes Jim to look outward rather than inward for the criteria by which he acts.

The consequences of flip-flopping are apparent in the following conversation about a plant manager named Ben. The conversation is between Will, a senior manager who reports to Ben, and Holly, who reports to Will.

Holly: I'm touring the plant with Ben tomorrow with the engineering technology council.

Will: That's great. Are you going to lecture him?

Holly: Yes. We decided in our meeting that it was just getting to the point that our expectations and his were so far off base, that nobody knew what in the hell we were doing. We thought we would tell him all the things we have done since we got organized and just let him tell us what it is he wants us to do. Hopefully, we'll get some decent direction instead of these cryptic notes [*laughs*] that come about once a week that say, "You should take a look at this." And then, "You should take a look at that." Whatever is the soup of the day.

Will: Are you getting frustrated? [*Laughs.*]

Holly: We're getting confused—because we can't ever meet his expectations because we don't know what they are. They change on a daily basis.

Will: Can I help you on any of that?

Holly: I don't think so. Probably after he tells us what it is he wants to do, it'll probably be so stupid [*laughs*] that I'll have to have you interpret why he thinks it's important for us to do that.

Will: I'll do my best.

Will seems sympathetic to Holly's unflattering portrait of his plant manager. Ben has a problem with flip-flopping, and he doesn't know it. Perhaps Ben has never been told that inconsistency is a problem of his. Perhaps he has been told, either in subtle or not-so-subtle ways and chosen to ignore it. Ben could use some self-assessment and a reality check.

Checking Your Frames Against Reality

Underreliance on context produces a tendency to make the data from a situation fit our mental models rather than formulate our models based on the data. As the adage says, if a hammer is the only tool, the tendency is to see everything as a nail. The law of the hammer may be an extreme characterization, yet there are individuals who so firmly hold their mental models that they ignore information that could change their model. In a perverse way, they interpret contradictory information as consistent with their model (Fiske and Taylor, 1991). Usually this occurs for people who hold extremely strong beliefs yet encounter mixed or inconclusive evidence of some kind.

One of our colleagues, a long-time organizational consultant, tells the story of a plant manager with whom he worked for many months. The plant manager had developed a mental model for unions that was conditioned by years of experience managing unionized plants. The beliefs that were a part of his model were that unions and their officers were evil, bad for business, and bad for the company. This plant manager had his unions-are-evil model in place when he encountered a new union president. True to the law of the hammer, the plant manager framed everything that the union president did as bad. As a result, in his mind, the union president was not to be trusted or even given the time of day. The plant manager approached every meeting with the union president with his hammer; he assumed that the president was going to get to him.

Interestingly, our colleague's mental model for the union president was not necessarily that he was "against the company" but rather that he was "for the union." The union president had high convictions and commitment to the union and was conditioned to fight for its interests. Our colleague, as a consultant in the situation, felt that a little kindness and positive regard might set a new course for the relationship. He advised the plant manager to develop more sensitivity to the context. Although the manager's perceptions of unions he had dealt with may have been justified, prejudging each situation to fit his mental model was highly ineffective.

Making Your Timing Appropriate

The timing of our framing attempts is not usually an issue, especially for those matters that are a part of the routine functioning of our jobs. But there are situations in which timing is critical, when, for example, the routines of everyday work life are punctuated by crises. Major equipment breaks down, an accident occurs on the job, employees walk out, a plant shuts down, massive layoffs are made, a parent company goes bankrupt, a hostile takeover is in the works.

Certain types of crises engender emotions in the people involved that other crises do not. A bankruptcy or hostile takeover has a different impact on employees than a strike. Leaders must learn to gauge people's emotions during periods of crises and to time framing attempts accordingly. If anxiety builds over the lack of information regarding the fate of the company and, by implication, individuals' jobs, leaders must be very proactive and seize every opportunity to frame events as they unfold or even before they unfold.

Proactive Framing

Mark Cohen, former chairman of the Lazarus department store chain, learned the usefulness of proactive framing and practiced it when Campeau Corporation, Lazarus's owner, declared bankruptcy. The bankruptcy caused great uncertainty and consternation in the Lazarus organization. Lazarus itself was not bankrupt, but it was placed under Chapter 11 due to its ownership by Campeau. When news first broke, there was a great deal of media coverage in the Southern Ohio and Indiana cities in which Lazarus stores were located.

Lazarus's managers sensed ahead of time that all of the publicity surrounding the Campeau collapse would become a major problem for them as employees began to worry about their own fate. In an attempt to stave off some of the employees' anxiety and concern for their future, Cohen timed his framing opportunities in two ways: he preempted bad news and kept people apprised of changes.

When awareness of Campeau's troubles surfaced, but before the press got wind of them, Cohen called a meeting for all employees and explained what was going to happen and why. Then he scheduled meetings every day during the crisis period. In these meetings, he explained to employees what they would be seeing in the press the next day and framed the true implications of what they would be reading. The meetings were open forums in which Cohen encouraged questions and appeared open and honest with his answers. Several employees remarked that they were all really surprised at how much he told them and how open he was about the entire situation.

Cohen was not required to be proactive at all in his communication with his employees. He could have let his people read about events in the newspaper and issue only brief internal memoranda to acknowledge or respond. Instead, he scheduled regular meetings in which he was able to continue his framing and preempt the press. The key to the successful management of this crisis was in large part the timing of his framing attempts. Cohen's proactive framing inoculated his employees against information or misinformation that they would receive in the next day's media reports. Framing events after they had been reported would not have been nearly as effective.

Retroactive Framing

If there are crises in which we must proactively frame events in an unfolding drama, there are also crises where a blow-by-blow attempt to manage meaning would not be prudent. These situations occur when there is a major conflict or where a dispute is transpiring and a "cooling-off" period becomes necessary in order for people to regain perspective. It is analogous to the aggressive but inexperienced television news reporters interviewing a couple as they watch their house go up in flames and asking the question, "Well, what does watching your house burn down mean to you folks?" The question seems ridiculous and insensitive; the answer, obvious. But the same question, asked sometime later to the same couple, could elicit a very different answer, depending upon the perspective they have gained in trying to reclaim their lives. Sometimes you just have to let the house burn down, just let events happen as they are destined to happen. And when perspective is regained, it is time for reflection and the management of meaning through the framing of events. This is *retroactive framing*.

The first author of this book (Gail Fairhurst) learned the value of a retroactive strategy during a strike by the University of Cincinnati faculty in the spring of 1993. As a department head, she found it difficult to know how to manage the meaning of the strike for a faculty that was deeply divided over the issue. The strike lasted for approximately one week, and ultimately it seemed that any public or departmental action must wait until the strike was over. The strike was settled early on the weekend, and the faculty returned on Monday to find the memo reproduced in Exhibit 4.1 in their mailboxes.

There were many positive reactions to this memorandum. But it is probable that receptivity was greater with retroactive framing than it would have been with proactive framing or framing in the midst of the strike when the bitterness was at its height. In the heat of a conflict, faculty members on opposing sides would have found it just too difficult to accept symbolic attempts to reinforce family ties. Thus, the timing was critical.

Preparing the Ground: Learn from Today's Experiences

"Should have, could have, would have . . . I should have framed it this way because . . . I could have framed it this way if only . . . I would have framed it that way, but . . ." When we are first becoming aware of the subject of framing, we may recognize constraints or great opportunities to manage meaning only after we have

Exhibit 4.1. Memo from Department Head to Faculty.

Date: April 5, 1993
To: All faculty, students, and staff
From: Gail Fairhurst
Re: Strike

This past week was one I hope never to repeat. I found it very upsetting to cross the picket lines. To those who were on the picket lines, I know you felt strongly for the cause that you were fighting for. To those faculty who chose not to strike, I know that some of you were very torn about this decision, others not. To those part-time faculty and graduate teaching assistants whose sympathies were with the striking faculty, but who were forced to teach because they were not legally protected, I know how hard the strike was on you as well. . . .

We work in an institution for which a diversity of opinion is encouraged and exists about every issue imaginable. The diversity of opinions about the faculty strike is no exception.

Our task now is not to sweep our deep feelings under the rug, but to acknowledge them and to speak about them as the occasion warrants. I was glad that Dr. Jordan wrote the memo expressing his views about the strike, and I encouraged those of you who commented on it to write or call him, because as a university community and an academic discipline, what we should be about is dialogue. But in doing so, I hope that all of us recognize, given the diversity of opinion about the strike, that ultimately we must agree to disagree.

Recently, it was suggested to me that the department functions in many ways like a family. Quite honestly, I don't think of the family metaphor in the trite terms that many organizations use regarding unconditional support or protection from outsiders. Raising three kids, and coming from a family of four siblings, I think of a family with members that we are unable to choose, members with whom we disagree and get mad at, members with responsibilities that are sometimes unevenly distributed, and members who must come to grips with the fact that they are part of a larger unit and must act with a sense of their interdependence.

We have so much work that we must accomplish if we are to remain a thriving academic unit. I ask you to keep this in mind as you resolve your own feelings about the strike. Good luck to you.

communicated with someone. Doubts, second guesses, and better comebacks—should have, could have, would have—strike as we are driving home from work, lying in bed at night, or waking up in the morning shower. Because most of our communications are so automatic, it may seem that becoming truly skilled at framing is just too difficult. All the opportunities we let slip by are most frustrating.

If you are thinking about those missed opportunities, take heart. Remember, our mental models are based upon our experiences and, importantly, what we pay attention to in those experiences. By replaying missed opportunities or ignored constraints, we imprint our unconscious minds with a message that says, in effect, "Take note. Remember this. Integrate this with what I already know." Whether we realize it or not, we have sensitized ourselves to an opportunity that may be gained in the future, and in that way we develop our mental models. Our second thoughts help us prepare the ground for future opportunities with the help of our unconscious minds and the process called priming (discussed in Chapter Seven). So use those refrains of should have, could have, would have. You will learn from your replayed experience.

This is an especially important message for leaders with a vision. As discussed earlier, visions are rarely rejected in one fell swoop. For a vision to take hold, it has to be integrated into the most routine aspects of our jobs. There are and should be countless opportunities to communicate the vision. Think of the numerous venues in which problems are discussed. Performance reviews, employee meetings, site visits, annual meetings, newsletters, interviews, briefings, "one-to-ones," mediations, and team meetings are just a few that can be named.

The authors of this book know a manager who, when an opportunity has passed him by to communicate about his vision, creates another opportunity by using whatever communication channel is available to redress the issue. Sometimes he brings his unit back together for another brief meeting. Other times he sends a brief e-mail message to specific unit members about "a point of clarification." He sends memos to the staff with some "reflective thoughts" about yesterday's session vis-à-vis the vision. He also drops by specific employees' offices just to say, "I didn't have the chance to say so yesterday, but I liked what you said about where we are," or, "You made me realize something about this vision of ours that I hadn't considered." Replaying those missed opportunities leads this manager to reclaim opportunities in any way possible.

A Backward Glance at This Chapter

The purpose of this chapter was to suggest that our framing effectiveness and context sensitivity are very closely linked. This discussion of the importance of context made the following points:

- Context is defined by those elements that shape how people think and what they expect. These elements are arranged in such a way that they take on a gestalt quality, so that the various parts are seen as a unified whole.
- Being insensitive to the context can be destructive. Without sensitivity to context, we remain unaware of the opportunities to affect our work environments through even simple framing of everyday work issues. A number of tools can help us become more sensitive to both the cultural and the business context.
- Particularly important is taking the time to know the culture, business environment, and surrounding events. This requires acquiring a certain base knowledge and then constantly keeping abreast of changes.
- Within the larger environment, it is important to know the people in the audience, their mental models, and the specific frames they hold. We can determine what frames people have by asking questions, testing whether their frames are permeable, and helping them find space for new thinking.
- With our own principles as an internal compass, we can find appropriate consistency and thus avoid the consequences of flip-flopping on issues and everyday questions.
- We need to be sure that our mental models are appropriate for the current circumstances and that we aren't responding in an outdated or inappropriate fashion.
- When we frame can be as important as what we frame. In some circumstances, proactive framing is vital; in others, retroactive framing is more productive. Be sure to assess each situation.

- We need to learn from our experiences, good and bad. Rather than let today's missed opportunity disappear over the horizon, we can refocus attention so that the opportunity is embraced.

These methods for navigating context can be a very great resource. Together with the powerful language tools for framing presented in the next chapter, they can help you use framing for stellar results.

Chapter Five

Tools for Framing
Metaphor, Jargon, Contrast, Spin, and Stories

Just as an artist works from a palette of colors to paint a picture, the leader who manages meaning works from a vocabulary of words and symbols to help construct a frame in the mind of the listener. And just as artists and leaders must be conscious of aesthetics, you must too. You can choose images that are rather common to build your frames, and you will likely get your message across. You can choose images that are blurry and indistinct and leave others guessing, as though they were trying to appreciate a tapestry from behind. Or you can choose images that are rich, distinctive, and memorable for the ways they crystallize understanding.

Designing Memorable Frames

In this chapter, we will explore five language forms that you can use to build memorable frames:

1. *Metaphors* will describe your subject's likeness to something else.
2. *Jargon* and *catchphrases* will frame your subject in familiar terms.
3. *Contrast* will illuminate your subject in terms of its opposite.
4. *Spin* will cast your subject in a positive or negative light.
5. *Stories* will make your subject more real by way of example.

Table 5.1 presents a brief description of what these forms mean, when to use them, and when to avoid them. The following sections elaborate on each form in turn.

Table 5.1. Framing Tools.

Type of Frame	Metaphors	Jargon/ Catch- phrases	Contrast	Spin	Stories
Function	They show a subject's likeness with some- thing else	They frame a subject in familiar terms.	It describes a subject in terms of its opposite.	It puts a subject in a positive or negative light.	They frame a subject by example.
Use it because	You want a subject to take on new meaning.	Familiar references can enhance meaning. Jargon and catchphrases help com- municate a vision's "god" and "devil" terms.	It is some- times easier to define what your subject is not than state what it is.	It can reveal your subject's strengths or weaknesses.	Stories attract attention and can build rapport.
Avoid it when	They mask important alternative meanings.	A word or phrase is in danger of overuse.	Meaning can be skewed by a poor contrast.	The ratio of spin to reality is excessive.	They mask important alternative meanings.
Example	"I feel our relationship is formal, like punch- ing a ticket."	"We've got to break the squares today."	"It's a choice between raising my hand for the teacher to ask if it's okay or just telling it like it is."	"Which Ray will show up? The one who's cooperative and gener- ous, or the egotist who constantly reminds others of his successes and what is due him."	"In my first three or four years here, I was a lot like you. I thought … "

Metaphors: Showing Likenesses

Linguists Lakoff and Johnson (1980, p. 3) tell us that metaphors are "pervasive in everyday life, not just in language but in thought and action." The late Sam Walton of Wal-Mart fame understood this intuitively. In his memoirs, he relayed how he viewed Wal-Mart's relationship to K-Mart. Walton was the quarterback on his high school's football team, which went undefeated and won the state championship. As he said, "In my whole life I never played in a losing football game. It taught me to expect to win. Later on in life, I think K-Mart, or whatever competition we were facing, just became Jeff City High School, the team we played for the state championship in 1935" (Walton and Huey, 1992, p. 14).

This example shows us how metaphors do more than just dress up our thoughts. Playing in a football game is not the same thing as competing against K-Mart. But Mr. Walton acted as though it were a game, relied on his experience of expecting to win, and framed the Wal-Mart and K-Mart competition in that way. Because we think with and through metaphors, they often surface as we frame for others.

Metaphors help us to understand and experience one thing in terms of another (Lakoff and Johnson, 1980). The pleasure we derive from them, however, comes from the novelty and surprise that we experience when a subject takes on new meaning. There is no better place to look for examples of this principle than in great literature. One of the reasons it gives us such pleasure is because of the richness of metaphorical images. Consider George Orwell's use of metaphor in his novel *Burmese Days,* as a major character talks about his murder of an elephant.

> I got up. The Burmans were already racing past me across the mud. It was obvious that the elephant would never rise again, but he was not dead. He was breathing very rhythmically with long rattling gasps, his great mound of a side painfully rising and falling. His mouth was wide open—I could see far down into caverns of pale pink throat. I waited a long time for him to die, but his breathing did not weaken. Finally, I fired my two remaining shots into the spot where I thought his heart must be. The thick blood welled out of him like red velvet, but still he did not die. His body did not

even jerk when the shots hit him, the tortured breathing continued without a pause. He was dying, very slowly and in great agony, but in some world remote from me where not even a bullet could damage him further. . . . The tortured gasps continued as steadily as the ticking of a clock [White, 1970, p. 192].

Metaphors such as "great mound of a side," "caverns of pale pink throat," and "blood . . . like red velvet" stay in our minds because of the images they evoke. Through the comparisons they draw, metaphors help us to think in new ways and, often, with more vividness and clarity.

In the same way that metaphors intrigue us in great literature, they can help us to think more concretely about concepts, processes, people, and objects at work. Consider the case of an antisocial manager. Bill is the kind of manager who avoids small talk or socializing at work. Charles, on the other hand, has always had managers that were friendly and approachable—that is, until he came to work for Bill.

(1) *Charles:* I feel like our relationship is so formal. We just come in, do the business, and leave. And it's like—

(2) *Bill:* Like punching a ticket.

(3) *Charles:* Yeah, like punching a ticket. We go an hour. Okay, hour's up. We're all done.

(4) *Bill:* Let me explain my feelings around social interactions with people at work. It is nothing, by the way, that concerns you personally. I don't socialize with anybody in the module, and I do that on purpose. Part of the team-building that we got into earlier was if you put more than two people in a room from this company, work is the only thing they would talk about. And I'll tell you right now, there's one individual in Kiwanis who I worked for at one time.

(5) *Charles:* Here?

(6) *Bill:* Yes, in this module. And it's very uncomfortable for me to deal with it.

(7) *Charles:* I understand. But I can feel a shield, a wall around you. I know that it's not me personally, but I feel that you're missing a lot.

Charles's and Bill's first statements are a wonderful illustration of how communicators co-construct meaning using metaphor. Notice how Charles struggles for the right words to describe their relationship. When Bill likens it to "punching a ticket," Charles subsequently agrees *(3)*. "Like punching a ticket" is a metaphorical expression known as a simile, in which two dissimilar things are compared by use of the words *like* or *as*. Charles goes on, however, to supply the shield and wall metaphors at the end of the excerpt to further describe Bill's self-imposed isolation *(7)*. This framing, too, demonstrates how metaphors can add more vividness and clarity to our thinking.

In the next example, John urges his direct report, Pete, to change his management style with the teams. John's feedback is consistent with the company's efforts to increase participative management through team-building and Total Quality Management.

(1) *John:* I'd like to talk with you about building personal relationships. My opinion is that many people don't understand you from a personal standpoint or a business standpoint. For some reason, people have this image of you as being very hard core, controlling, and insensitive, and I don't think that's true.

(2) *Pete:* Yeah.

(3) *John:* I think that you're real sensitive, but sometimes you're unwilling to share that sensitivity with others. You need to open yourself up to people because it's a lot easier for them to understand that you're caring and that you want to do what's right for the business and for them.

(4) *Pete:* With technicians or team leaders, I always look for their suggestions and their input. I rarely make decisions for people. But somehow the work team sees me this way. The first time I realized it was at our off-site. Smith said he saw me as very controlling, very direct. It shocked me. I went home and told my wife, Peg, and she laughed.

(5) *John:* [*Laughs.*]

(6) *Pete:* So, to me, it's really two different faces.

There is great economy in word choice with metaphors, and we can see this in Pete's metaphor, "two different faces." He was referring to the very different image that the team had of him as compared to his own self-image, which was seen only by his wife and John. The "two different faces" metaphor instantly calls to mind several possible meanings: Pete has multiple personas; others' perceptions of him differ sharply; he reveals different parts of himself in different situations; and his surface image is not necessarily the real Pete. These meanings are so central to the metaphorical image of "two faces" that they do not require Pete to explain them in any more detail.

John also uses metaphor to frame Pete's current image as "hard core" *(1)* and to frame a desired image, one in which Pete would "open . . . up" *(3)*. Obviously, a person's image can never be hard or open in a literal sense, but Pete's real and desired images are more clearly defined when these terms are applied to them.

A metaphor is one type of analogy; it is an *implied analogy*. A *literal analogy* draws a comparison between two clearly similar things such as Harvard and Yale. A *figurative analogy* draws a comparison between two apparently dissimilar things such as a business organization and a family. Often, we need look no further than the editorial pages to find examples of excellent analogies, usually from the world of politics. Maureen Dowd, of the *New York Times* (1993), drew an analogy between Bill Clinton and the cartoon character of Wimpy in writing about the early days of the Clinton presidency: "'I cannot recommend this year, although I expect to recommend in this term, tax relief for middle-income families, especially those with children,' he told the *Cincinnati Enquirer.* Spoken by a president who is trying to push through Congress a huge tax increase, that suggestion raised an unfortunate echo of Wimpy, friend of Popeye: 'I will gladly pay you Tuesday, sir, for a hamburger today.'"

Likening Clinton to Wimpy was a biting comparison, the kind indeed that most political pundits intend. Like a biting or stirring metaphor, a good analogy will produce meaning through a novel and surprising comparison of two subjects. However, this example also points to another very important point about metaphors and analogies. When one thing is seen in terms of another, it limits our experience with the first thing because it hides or distracts us from other potentially meaningful aspects of the concept we are trying to introduce (Lakoff and Johnson, 1980). For example, before being compared to Wimpy, Clinton had been known as "Slick Willie," a reference to his ability to fast-talk his way out of political jams. The use of the Wimpy analogy distracts us from the image of Bill Clinton as a fast talker.

Of course, intentionally hiding another meaning is exactly what we may intend. Consider a rather heated discussion that ensued between Randy, a warehouse manager, and Al, who reports to him. They are discussing a job consolidation in the warehouse; Al favors it, Randy does not. Randy uses a rather inflammatory frame of the job consolidation, which makes his position seem morally right and Al's position seem morally wrong.

(1) *Randy:* Philosophically, when the jobs were broken up, people got more pay. Now that we're combining them again, people are going to get more pay. Every time you make a change, people are going to get more pay. Why? The work remains exactly the same. We are bastardizing our job evaluation system if we make this change, which I don't want to do. I want to hold that [system] in high regard.

(2)   *Al:* When I look at it, I say, gee, are we bastardizing our job evaluation system or is what we're doing wise? The fact is, we would be moving them up not blatantly but officially.

Note the verbal play around the "bastardizing" metaphor *(1)*. Something that is bastardized is illegitimate or impure, with hints at the immoral. To accept this metaphor is to automatically rule out making the change being discussed, because bastardizing is so reprehensible. Al recognizes this and sets out to reframe "bastardizing" with "wise" and "not blatant but official," framing intended to produce more positive meanings *(2)*.

No doubt Randy felt justified in using strong wording because he perceived Al's position to be harmful. However, this metaphor could also be perceived as an overly negative, manipulative framing of Al's position. Randy had a reputation for being very control oriented and using a wide range of manipulative verbal tactics, including exaggeration, to get his way.

Just where we draw the line between influence and manipulation rests upon our personal values and is, ultimately, a judgment call. But the deeds of manipulative framers, like Randy, eventually catch up with them. Instead of inspiring trust and confidence, they create distrust and suspicion. Instead of building relationships, they tear them down. Like Al, others are not blind to the use of language tools that allow manipulators to hide and highlight a subject to suit only their interests.

The tendency of metaphors and analogies to favor certain aspects of experience and hide others was the subject of John Clancy's (1989) book about the metaphors of the major business leaders of the last two centuries. In writing about the key metaphors of business, he cautions, "[A] poor metaphor applied to business can have enormously harmful effects when actions are based on a mistaken analogy. For these are not merely fanciful and playful verbal tricks; these are ideas that ground our experience and determine our actions. We take a very concrete concept, with all of its implications, and apply it to something else that may resemble the original concept in some ways but surely is not identical with it" (p. 27).

Like Lakoff and Johnson (1980), Clancy argues that we must examine the relationships and concepts that metaphors bring to mind. We must make sure the application is a good one and that there are no clashes between our combination of metaphors with other metaphors or language, our behavior, and others' expectations. Metaphors are powerful tools whose implied relationships must be carefully considered.

We must also be aware that the heavy use of particular metaphors results in their losing the novelty and surprise they once held. When metaphors have been used so often that they have lost their vividness, they are considered clichés (Thomas, 1969). An implicit recognition of this fact is that, when using clichés, we often apologize for them, as in, "It's a cliché, but it's not over till the fat lady sings," or, "Cliché or not, we really are a family here."

Dead metaphors, too, have lost their original punch. They are different from clichés, however, in that there is no longer any metaphorical intent because their meanings have become accepted as standard. For example, in his book on metaphors, Owen Thomas (1969, p. 64) writes that the word *agony* (from the Greek) originally signified a struggle for victory in ancient athletic games. *Expedite* (from the Latin) originally meant to free a person caught by the foot. *Symposium* (from the Greek) was originally a drinking party. These meanings, which once gave these words metaphoric depth of meaning, are lost to us.

Though metaphors have their limitations and risks, we should not underestimate the power of metaphor to help us with our framing strategies. In the exploration of several more language tools in the following pages, we will see that metaphors are frequently used in conjunction with these tools. Quite simply, metaphors are essential to our ability to think and describe.

Jargon and Catchphrases: Enhancing Meaning with Familiar References

Jargon is language that is peculiar to a particular profession, an organizational culture, or a well-developed vision or program. A *catchphrase* is a common expression that comes from our everyday language or the language of the organization. Catchphrases can be jargon, but they are also colloquialisms, slogans, or slang (such as "hit the sack," "anytime, anywhere, anything," "techies"). Both jargon and catchphrases are summary statements about a subject that suggest a general framing of it (Gamson and Lasch, 1983). They are appealing language choices because they bring a very familiar and accepted meaning to the subject with which they are associated. Sometimes they contain metaphors, other times they do not.

Raymond Smith of Bell Atlantic observed how the jargon changed in his organization when an internal communications program called the Bell Atlantic Way was introduced (Kanter, 1991). Exercises in employee-training sessions, such as "breaking the squares" and "finding the blue chips," became Bell Atlantic symbols as they made their way into the everyday language of employees. "We've got to break the squares today" stood for compromise and the need to find new ways of thinking. When "focusing on the blue chips" or "blue chip assignment" was heard, an important task was being designated, and others were expected to know it was a priority. Jargon emerged out of a common experience base in training exercises, and in everyday conversation it became a reminder of Bell Atlantic Way principles.

In Chapter Two, we said that a well-developed vision will often supply a set of "god," "devil," and "good" terms. These terms often translate to specific jargon, slogans, or theme statements (for example, the theme of *quality* in TQM). The jargon that a vision supplies can and should be used frequently in conversation, because such use constitutes repeated framing and reinforcement of the vision. Avoidance of an awkward or inappropriate use of the jargon is, of course, critical for clear communication about the vision. Consider the following statement:

Sue: I felt that the work teams which they participated in were filled with people doing their best—you know, willing workers.

And another:

Mory: That computer, which will control chart it for us, tells us if something is going out. We will pay attention to that rather than the finished product test.

These statements present two examples of "good" terms from TQM that have been effectively incorporated into the everyday speech of the users. The use of the "good" terms *willing workers* and *control chart* to frame everyday work events helps others to see the vision as a natural and implicitly accepted part of the work context.

Catchphrases creep into our language from all kinds of sources. Remember Iraqi leader Saddam Hussein's reference to "the mother of all battles"? In his book *War Slang: American Fighting Words and Phrases from the Civil War to the Gulf War,* author Paul Dickson (1994) chronicles the catchphrases of war. He notes how Hussein's catchphrase was picked up and used by Defense Secretary Dick Cheney, who remarked that Saddam Hussein fathered "the mother of all retreats." The *Boston Globe* noted that Hussein had painted himself into "the mother of all corners." Finally, General H. Norman Schwarzkopf's final briefing at the end of the war became known as "the mother of all briefings." While Hussein's use of the phrase was intended to denote size and importance, the Americans' use of the phrase was clearly to ridicule.

A creative use of catchphrases characterized the protest groups in an environmental controversy over a $160 million hazardous waste–destruction facility, located in East Liverpool, Ohio. This facility is owned and operated by Waste Technologies Industries (WTI). As the East Liverpool–WTI incinerator controversy heads into its third decade, the story is a familiar one. Some residents want to see this facility operate because it can help rejuvenate an aging town with a sluggish economy. Other residents, however, oppose its operation because it is built on an aquifer that supplies drinking water, and it is in close proximity to schools and privately owned homes. After an EPA disclosure in October 1992 that the agency could not stop operations at WTI, a number of community groups went on the offensive. Note the framing with catchphrases in the names of the protesting groups (Case, 1993):

- A group of grandparents identified themselves as *The Grand Eight* and chained themselves to the gates of the facility.
- Five medical professionals named themselves *The Band-Aid Bunch* and also chained themselves to the gates.
- Ten union members called themselves *The Von Roll Shut-Down Team* and constructed a cinder block wall in front of the facility. (Von Roll is the name of WTI's parent company.)
- Other groups framed themselves as *The Parent Trap Eleven* and *The American Dream Team Five*.

Each group coined a catchphrase to frame itself. The phrases were familiar and culturally recognizable yet applied in novel ways. And therein lies their appeal.

While familiarity is often a strength, it can also be a weakness. When overused, expressions turn people off and lose their effectiveness. Several years ago, a service organization in the South (not one in the communications industry) had a major internal communication campaign that produced the slogan, "We're a communicating company." The slogan was everywhere—on posters, on business cards, on letterhead, in house organs. The slogan was used repeatedly by management to explain almost any business activity or decision. "Communicating" took on so many different meanings that it came to have no meaning at all.

Contrast: Using Opposites or Alternatives to Define

It bears repeating that the concepts around which we manage meaning are often vague and ambiguous. As a language tool, contrast is very useful because sometimes we can say what our subject is not more easily than we can say what it is. Consider the following conversation between Jolene and Dan, both of whom are team leaders. They are talking about another manager in the module, named Peter.

(1) *Jolene:* Whenever I have talked to him about something, if I really push against him, he'll give in. Then he'll go off and do what he wants to do anyways. And I don't really want to call it an honesty issue because I don't think that's really where he's coming from.

(2) *Dan:* Two things about Peter that I have picked up. One is that he lacks confidence.

(3) *Jolene:* Yeah, that makes sense. That's why I don't want to call it an honesty issue. I feel like he's got the right answers a lot of times, but if it is people oriented, he won't even challenge me. If it is technology, he just doesn't talk, period.

(4) *Dan:* Mm-hmm. The other thing is that he works awful hard. So he may feel that he can't take the time.

(5) *Jolene:* He does go a mile a minute.

(6) *Dan:* Oh yeah. And it always looks like he's had three or four cups of something [*laughs*].

Jolene can describe Peter's behavior; she cannot characterize what motivates him and so uses contrast to indicate what she would rule out. This dialogue also presents a good example of the co-construction of meaning: Jolene finds help from Dan as he frames Peter's problem as "a lack of confidence" *(2, 3)*. It also shows the use of a catchphrase ("mile a minute") to frame Peter's frenetic style *(5)*.

Contrast can be achieved in two basic ways. We can contrast a subject with its opposite or with one, two, or more alternatives. In the following example, Tony uses both forms of contrast as he instructs his direct report, Norm, about a team complaint.

(1) *Tony:* You might want to pursue this headache complaint that the team is making to see if there is some justification for it. I don't know what the solution might be, but don't turn a deaf ear to it.

(2) *Norm:* I'm not going to.

(3) *Tony:* But I would suggest that you make sure and differentiate between a safety issue and a work performance
issue. Do that real clearly.

(4) *Norm:* Yes. Okay, all right.

Note that Tony wants Norm to listen to what the team is saying.
He frames the opposite behavior and cautions against it. Tony also
uses contrast when he instructs Norm to "differentiate between a
safety issue and a work performance issue" *(3)*. His contrast frames
two alternatives—in this case, types of problems.

When a person is framing two or more alternatives, a preference for one over the other will often be stated. In the following
example, Ben is a young manager who expresses his desire to make
more decisions on his own. He contrasts this goal with his usual
decision-making style.

(1) *Ben:* I need to make more decisions without always making
sure that I consult with you. A lot of it is my mind-set,
how I put my thoughts together when I present them
to you.

(2) It's two different perspectives, like, "Hey, is this okay?"
versus "This is what I want to do. I'm going to go do it
unless you tell me, and I'll stop." The endpoint is the
same, but it's like, raise my hand for the teacher and
ask, "Is it okay?" or just tell it like it is.

(3) *Tom:* Good. That's a good example. I want you to say to me,
"This is what I think is right. This is what I want to do
and what I need to do to meet my goals."

(4) I want you to manage me as your boss to help you
accomplish what you want to do versus giving me the
opportunity to say, "Well, I don't know. Maybe we'll do
that sometime."

Both managers effectively use contrast in this example. Both
of them frame Ben's preferred and usual styles of management
through the typical dialogue that represents these styles. Ben's preference *(1)* is clearly helped along by the contrast that he is able to
present *(2)*.

In the 1988 presidential campaign, Jesse Jackson rose to prominence as a presidential candidate. He did so with some powerful language in which he blended contrast with metaphor. For example, in a speech before a mixed-race crowd in South Carolina, he said, "It's not so much black versus white as it is barracudas eating us small fish. They don't eat fish by color. They eat fish by size." Jackson successfully turned heads in that campaign with rich language of this nature. Here, his contrast and metaphor successfully refuted a race frame held by a white constituency and replaced it with a socioeconomic frame. For many people during that election, including an unlikely constituency of white Midwestern farmers, Jackson was able to neutralize race as a factor.

But contrast is not without its downside. Because a subject draws meaning by virtue of what we choose as its contrasting factor, a cautionary note is required. Let's stay with Jesse Jackson as an example. If we contrast Jesse Jackson with Louis Farrakhan, an outspoken Black Muslim leader, then Jesse Jackson looks moderate. However, if we contrast Jesse Jackson with David Duke, former member of the Ku Klux Klan and Louisiana politician, then Jesse Jackson looks quite liberal. Since a poor contrast can skew meaning in an undesirable direction, the choice of contrast makes a real difference in the assignment of meaning. And, as we will see next, contrast is often used with spin.

Spin: Revealing Strengths and Weaknesses

In the past decade or so, presidential politics has given us a new term, *spin*. Those who practice the art are called *spin doctors*. The spin doctors of political campaigns or public relations interpret their candidate's performance in positive terms and the opposing candidate's performance in negative terms.

The translation of spin to a business environment is obvious and has been around as long as public affairs departments. Only the term is new. In fact, spin is a very common framing tool in everyday business language. With *positive spin,* a subject is seen in terms of its strengths. With *negative spin,* a subject is seen in terms of its weaknesses.

When former Merck CEO P. Roy Vagelos outlined his vision for the acquisition of Medco, a bold move that changed the pharmaceutical industry, he cast both a positive and a negative spin on the situation.

Positive Spin   Medco gives us the ability to link different parts of the health care–delivery system. The result is what we call coordinated pharmaceutical care, which could save billions of dollars a year in health care costs in the United States through the prevention of inappropriate drug interactions, undermedication, and overmedication. A study by Sharon Wilcox, David Himmelstein, and Steffie Woolhandler, published this summer in the *Journal of the American Medical Association,* shows that one in four elderly people is taking inappropriate medicines. Studies also indicate that one of every two patients who need prescription drugs for chronic conditions such as high blood pressure and elevated cholesterol simply stops taking medication after one year. We can solve these problems [Nichols, 1994, p. 106].

Negative Spin   One danger, of course, is that scientists and managers may become overwhelmed by all this information and the possibilities it presents. At Merck, we must be able to condense reams of information and let our best judgment, and not our worst fears, prevail [p. 106].

Positive Spin   At the end of the day, in pharmaceuticals or any other business, you've got to be able to place your bets. Merck has done that by buying Medco: we made a $6.6 billion bet on where the future of the industry lies. It's an awfully big bet, but I believe that the company that best controls the information flow from doctor to patient to pharmacist to plan sponsor has the best chance of succeeding in this industry [p. 106].

Vagelos's strategy to spin first positive, then negative, then positive again is a wise one. All visions have an up side and a down side, and the more aware listeners are of all possibilities, the more they can plan for the contingencies that surface in implementation. Moreover, the positive-negative-positive spin cycle sells the

vision and acknowledges its negative side and yet keeps the audience from focusing too much on the negatives by redirecting
attention back to the positives at the end.

The obvious cautionary note when using spin concerns the
amount. The journalists who covered the spin doctors from the
1988 presidential campaign made this point, most pointedly, in
comments after the Lloyd Bentsen–Dan Quayle debate (Brydon,
1989):

> We reporters were more than just spun tonight, we were twirled, we
> were twisted, we were Cuisinarted.
>
> —*Leslie Stahl, CBS*

> If a spin controller told me that the sun was shining, and I was
> outside and the sun was shining, I'd call the weather bureau.
>
> —*Jeff Greenfield, ABC*

> There was so much spinning going on here tonight, it's a wonder
> that Omaha Civic Auditorium didn't lift off into orbit.
>
> —*Tom Brokaw, NBC*

There are two sides to every story, of course. If the press cries
foul for too positive a portrayal of a candidate, the politicians cry
foul for the press's too negative portrayal. This is nicely demonstrated in an editorial by Michael Kinsley in the *New Yorker* (1995).
On January 5, 1995, testifying before the House Ways and Means
Committee, House Speaker Newt Gingrich proposed a tax credit for
welfare recipients so they could buy laptop computers. Kinsley uses
contrast to show both the positive and negative spins of Gingrich:

> Gingrich himself labeled the laptop tax credit "a nutty idea," but he
> was using the word "nutty" in its modern, self-congratulatory sense,
> in which insanity is linked with creativity and freedom from con-
> vention. The Speaker was projecting his preferred image of himself
> as pixie-like and imaginative (as opposed to his critics' preferred
> image of him as nasty and calculating). Also high-tech and future-
> oriented (as opposed to old-fashioned and backward-looking).
> Also, of course, full of generous feelings towards the poor (as
> opposed to Ebenezer Scrooge–like) [p. 6].

How you will respond to Kinsley's depiction depends in part upon your vantage point. In general, spinning produces a negative response when the amount of spin begins to depart substantially from the perceived reality of the subject targeted for meaning. In other words, when the spin-to-fact ratio becomes disproportionate, then credibility is lost. No amount of positive spin will enhance the image of a candidate who blows a debate. Likewise, no amount of spin will alter the meaning of an event for others who are informed and able to evaluate the event's positive and negative aspects.

Here is an example from an organization that the authors studied. Cathy is a department manager, and Ernie is a longtime employee who reports to her. As part of his responsibility, Ernie must coordinate his efforts with another function headed by Jamieson. Note Cathy's response to Ernie's negative spin of Jamieson.

Cathy: How did your meeting go with Jamieson?

Ernie: Well, my opinion of him just keeps getting worse and worse. I swear this guy will show up late to his own funeral and have a set of excuses a mile long when he meets his maker.

Cathy: Come on, Ernie, aren't you exaggerating maybe a little? I'm not saying that I like what's going on any more than you. But it's only been this project that he hasn't delivered for us. If he doesn't have the personnel over there like he used to, then there's going to be delays.

Ernie: Well, you might be right. But if it was my shop, I'd find a way to make good on what I promised or get with my boss to see the problems this is causing. I don't care who's at fault, we're losing money every day he doesn't deliver.

Cathy: No question there.

Note that Cathy questions Ernie's framing, suggesting it may be an exaggeration. In Cathy's view, the amount of Ernie's spin is disproportionate to her take on Jamieson's situation.

Stories: Making It Real

A final framing tool for managing meaning through language is storytelling. Have you ever noticed how people seem to settle down and listen carefully when a story is being told? Stories engage our attention because they are often about the problems that people experience and the resolutions they work out. Stories are much larger linguistic units than metaphors, jargon, catchphrases, contrast, or spin. Often, they include several of these language forms as they relate to a particular story line. Thus, a single story could manage meaning around several subjects. Usually, however, there is a central theme or subject whose meaning is to be established through an example.

TRW's Frederick C. Crawford was a renowned storyteller who guided the company through many management and manufacturing transitions until the late 1950s (Dyer, 1991). When asked about using stories as a communications strategy, he commented about the ability of a story to make a point:

> A few years ago on a street in Cleveland, I ran into a woman who had worked for us during the war. After we exchanged greetings, she recalled a story I had told at one of the mass meetings years before. She had forgotten the circumstances, but she remembered the story. It was about cooperation: I was talking about the need to plan and work together. In those days, everybody used analogies from football, but I thought those stories were old and overworked even then.
>
> So I told a story about little Willie, who wears short pants but wants long pants like the big boys, and Christmas is coming. He tells Santa Claus that he wants long pants. Mother gets him long pants, but they are about six inches too long, and she doesn't have time to fix them. She and Willie's sister and grandmother wrap them up and put them in a box under the Christmas tree. Mother puts the lights out and goes to bed and then starts thinking, "Poor little Willie, he'll be so disappointed that he can't wear his long pants Christmas Day." So about midnight, she gets up and goes downstairs, turns on the lights, cuts the six inches off the pants, hems them, and goes back to bed. At about one o'clock, grandmother does the same thing. At about two o'clock, sister does it again. The next morning, little Willie tries on his new pants, and they're even shorter than his old ones.
>
> The story is now dated, of course, but at the time it got a good laugh. It made the point that effort is fine, but you need cooperation to harness that effort. I had spoken for about 20 minutes, but 40 years later, this woman remembered that story. That tells you something.

Stories often make us laugh, as this one did Crawford's employees, because their messages can ring so true in our lives. For that reason, they help build rapport between speaker and listener. We can see another example of this if we return to the conversation between Pete and John, which appeared earlier in the chapter. John used the "hard core" metaphor to frame Pete's management style, while Pete acknowledged that his own work image was different from his self-image. He framed this split image as "two different faces." In a continuation of the conversation, John related a story about himself in which he indicated how similar he was to Pete when he was a young manager.

John: The other data point I have is that some people outside the department made remarks about your controlling behavior. A group manager said, "We ought to put Pete in Industrial Relations to soften him up some."

Pete: [*Laughs.*]

John: So, other people have this hard-core image.

Pete: Well, there's probably some validity.

John: You carry a tremendous load for the module. I know you have a lot of irons in the fire, and you work long and hard. I don't want to tell you to stop doing that, but to some degree you have to in order to establish relationships. I think that you can achieve a better balance.

   In my first three or four years, I was a lot like you. I thought if I wasn't busy, I wasn't contributing. I got a lot of feedback from secretaries especially. I would go in and say, "Here's what I want. Don't ask me how I'm doing today. Don't give me any of this chit-chat about what the weather's like cause I'm here for business. And that's why you're here, too, by the way."

Pete: [*Laughs.*]

John: They told me that I acted like they were the lowest people on the totem pole, and I never intended that. But in the way that I behaved, that's the image that they had of me.

Pete: I think I do that with the work team. I guess that's what I'm hearing. [*Silence.*]

This story enables John to skillfully frame himself as "I was like you" for Pete. He enhances Pete's chances of identifying with him and following the course of change that John charted for himself. And therein lies the power of stories. They get our attention. They can be compelling and move us to think in new ways. They engage our emotions. They help us to identify with one another and build rapport. In short, they are powerful exemplars of the points we wish to make.

Stories can also provide concrete examples of implicit assumptions that guide decision making and action (Wilkins, 1983). In the following example, Bert uses a story about a recent predicament to establish for Gary, his direct report, the need for TQM.

(1) *Gary:* I know I can impact the process control.

(2) *Bert:* And why is that true? I got a real good example for you that just came up on execution of the quality system. Yesterday, I get a call from Chuck Smith. He wants me on a rush basis to get him twenty-five cases of product. We sent them some product. It turns out it's got problems with—

(3) *Gary:* Cracked cores?

(4) *Bert:* No, not cracked cores, but tack down. So then I got enough data. Eli went and got the records. Sure enough, in that data were deviations for tack down. Okay. Then he put two and two together, and it was pretty easy to see there was a problem with that all day.

(5) *Gary:* Really?

(6) *Bert:* Well, it's a clear case of not executing properly. The system was okay, but we hadn't done the job here. Okay, so what has he done? What does it cost us?

(7) Well, first of all if it hadn't been for this incident where we got feedback from our own sources, we would have ticked off some consumer who might not buy the product again after it wouldn't have worked. And the other thing is, how often do we lament spending one, two, three days following up on screwups? Executing the quality system shortens that significantly. You probably have other real-life experiences that show the need for that [quality system].

Bert begins his story with a predicament and then reviews the steps he and his co-worker took to correct the problem. Not so coincidentally, these steps happen to be a role model for a TQM solution to the problem through the use of data-based analyses. The story thus reveals how a decision was made in this situation. Bert frames the source of the problem as "not executing [the quality system] properly" and then engages in positive spin over the TQM solution that got them out of this jam. Positive spin begins after the statement, "What does it cost us?" *(6)*. This example nicely combines a story with positive spin used to flesh out its meaning.

Just as metaphors can emphasize one aspect of a targeted event and hide another, so too can stories. During his time at General Motors, John DeLorean reportedly told the following story:

> In preparing for the sales official's trip to this particular city, the Chevrolet zone sales people learned from Detroit that the boss liked to have a refrigerator full of cold beer, sandwiches, and fruit in his room to snack on at night before going to bed. They lined up a suite in one of the city's better hotels, rented a refrigerator, and ordered food and beer. However, the door to the suite was too small to accommodate the icebox. The hotel apparently nixed a plan to rip out the door and part of the adjoining wall. So the quick-thinking zone people hired a crane operator, put them on the roof of the hotel, knocked out a set of windows in the suite, and lowered and shoved the refrigerator into the room through this gaping hole.
>
> That night the Chevrolet executive wolfed down cold-cut sandwiches, beer, and fresh fruit, no doubt thinking, "What a great bunch of people we have in this zone." The next day he was off to another city and most likely another refrigerator, while back in the city of his departure the zone people were once again dismantling hotel windows and removing the refrigeration by crane [Wright, 1979, p. 37].

In evaluating this story, it helps to know that it was common practice at GM to go overboard in deference to the wishes of those in authority (Martin and Siehl, 1983). This story could be told by individuals within the existing culture as testimony to the ingenuity required and the lengths to which one must go in order to please higher-ups. In the hands of John DeLorean, however, the meaning favored was the ridiculousness of it all. One can well imagine how the story could be repeated in conversation with weight given to either meaning. As with metaphor, certain meanings can be favored while others can be hidden or marginalized.

Putting the Tools to Use

Now you've seen the various tools for designing frames. But how do you actually use them? How can you learn the craft and art of putting them together and really making them yours? One of the best exercises that we have found for developing language skills comes from Genie Laborde's *Fine Tune Your Brain* (1988). It begins by asking that you discover a key metaphor. Once you have found the right metaphor, you can eventually incorporate all of the framing tools. The exercise also lends itself to framing an organizational vision.

The first step is to decide which meaning you wish to manage. Choose a "present state" problem and a "desired state" goal or vision. List the key elements of those points that are necessary for another person to understand the present and desired circumstances of both states. They will be the specific points about which you will manage meaning.

The second step is to formulate a set of parallel elements, the language forms (such as metaphors, jargon, catchphrases, contrast, spin, and stories) that can be used to portray the ideas or concepts relevant to your key elements. Because metaphors often structure how we think, start first with the metaphors that might parallel the key elements of your present and desired states.

Uncover a Complex Metaphor

Laborde recommends looking for what she calls a complex metaphor. A complex metaphor is a very useful communication tool because it has many implied aspects that can form "an intricate organization of parallel elements" (Laborde, 1988, p. 85). Complex metaphors allow us to influence others on an unconscious level as long as we are careful to dovetail the implied meanings of our metaphor with others' expected meanings. If the meanings are too disparate or jarring, people will probably resist, perhaps completely unconsciously, the comparison that we draw.

A good example of discovering and using a complex metaphor

was provided by the managers of public affairs at the Fernald plant, the site of an environmental cleanup located about twenty miles from Cincinnati. Fernald's public affairs program is a joint effort of the public affairs staff of the Department of Energy and that of the Fernald Environmental Restoration Management Corporation (FERMCO), a subsidiary of Fluor Daniel of Irvine, California. The Fernald plant produced uranium metal products for the nation's defense programs between 1953 and 1989. Here is how the members of the public affairs program discovered a complex metaphor when they sought to change the way they functioned.

Fernald's public affairs staff were highly motivated to avoid a continuation of a contentious history with stakeholders. They took a hard look at their present situation, one they had inherited from previous operators of the plant, and did not like what they saw. To begin with, historically, senior management had handed the entire responsibility of communicating with the public to public affairs, which remained the public's only information resource. Moreover, the communication between public affairs and Fernald's various stakeholders tended to be one-way, with very little real dialogue. These conditions reflect the key elements of the "present state" (see Table 5.2).

A small group of managers in the public affairs program tried

Table 5.2. Key Elements of Public Affairs at Fernald.

Present State	Desired State
The public affairs program is the only public information resource.	The public affairs program is a truly effective public information resource.
Communicating with the public is a "handoff" by senior management to public affairs.	Senior management accepts that public communication is its responsibility as well as that of public affairs.
Communicating with the public is one-way; two-way communication is lacking and results in a loss of public trust and confidence.	Two-way communication vehicles, such as the envoy program, are developed.

to envision what a more desirable future would look like for them. That depiction focused first on reaffirming the normal duties of public affairs, which included, among other responsibilities, public meetings, workshops, monthly reports, newsletters, and videos. Second, they wanted senior management to accept and own its responsibility to communicate with the public. Third, they wanted more two-way communication with the public, in keeping with Department of Energy policies that emerged in the 1990s. The most important step taken in support of this third element was the development of an envoy program. "Envoys" were Fernald employees who became members of various stakeholder organizations. Through its employees, Fernald hoped to foster more one-to-one dialogue with its stakeholders. These conditions reflect the key elements of the "desired state" (Table 5.2).

As the public affairs managers surveyed the key elements of their present and desired states, they were struck by two features of the desired future state. First, all three elements of their desired future seemed equal and interdependent. Second, the overriding goal for all three elements was the public's trust and confidence. A manager in the group then came up with the complex metaphor of a three-legged stool, and immediately the group was struck by the correspondence to the desired state; these parallels are outlined in Table 5.3.

The symbolic value of the three-legged stool—and the part that works directly on the unconscious mind—involves the implied meanings of *interdependence* and *support*. The center seat, or goal, is the public's trust and confidence. Each leg of the stool corresponds to a different aspect of the future state: public affairs information, senior management buy-in, and person-to-person communication.

The three metaphorical legs are themselves linked to one another, as is the case with many a three-legged stool; the legs and support for the seat are thus strengthened. The link between the public affairs program and the envoys is conceived primarily as one of training the envoys in how to be good listeners. Information management is the key link between envoys and managers; public affairs sees this as key to ensuring effective upward and downward communication. Finally, public affairs and management are linked by counseling, the communication planning support that public affairs wants to offer senior management.

Table 5.3 Parallel Components of Metaphor and Desired State.

Desired State	Three-Legged Stool
Public trust and confidence	Center seat
Public affairs program: a public information resource	First leg
Management buy-in	Second leg
Envoy program and two-way communication	Third leg
Training	Leg support between public affairs and the envoys
Information management	Leg support between management and the envoys
Counseling	Leg support between public affairs and management

Whenever managers in the public affairs program discuss their vision, they begin with the complex metaphor of the three-legged stool. It quickly becomes apparent that the implied meanings associated with a three-legged stool dovetail beautifully with the three interrelated goals of the vision.

Public affairs managers also tell the story of how the stool metaphor came into being, and through the negative spin of what was an undesirable present state, they create a sense of urgency for their proposed change. They have coined their own jargon in the naming of the envoys. They use contrast quite effectively to clarify the meaning of the envoys, as people whose goals are to "see and listen" and not to "tell and sell." Finally, they use positive spin in naming the anticipated outcomes of the coordinated set of programs they have instituted. The three-legged stool metaphor was critical in helping to clarify their thinking and their subsequent ability to manage the meaning of and interrelationship between their various programs.

Discover Strengths

The secret to the success of this exercise is the discovery of a complex metaphor. The only way to become skillful at finding a complex metaphor is through trial and error and, much as the Fernald people did, constant talking with others to flesh out possible new meanings for a subject. The results may be surprising. A big coffee grinder seems an unlikely candidate for a complex metaphor, but this is what Frederick Crawford of TRW used to show that human capital is a company's most important asset: "What do we put in the coffee grinder? We put in money and oil and steel and taxes and . . . labor . . . we put in all the ingredients and then added time. I would say to employees, 'Now Joe and Mary and Pete, and all of you, put in your eight hours and you help us, we'll get a hell of a lot out, and we'll divide the loot. Everybody will be better off—customers, suppliers, investors, and employees'" (Dyer, 1991, p. 121).

Comparing leadership in organizations to leading a caravan in the desert also seems an unlikely image, but international management experts Hans Hinterhuber and Wolfgang Popp (1992, p. 106) were struck by the parallels when they wrote about the value of possessing an organizational vision:

> The leader of a caravan in the desert, where sandstorms constantly change the landscape, looks to the patterns of the stars in the sky to stay on course. The stars are not the destination, but they do provide dependable guides for the journey to the next oasis, no matter which direction the caravan comes from, how well it is equipped for the trip, or how rough the terrain may be. Of course, the stars may point the way, but any Bedouin who hopes to reach the oasis safely knows to keep one eye on the ground to avoid quicksand—and to trust his caravan leader's sense of orientation.
>
> Like the North Star, a manager's vision is not a goal. Rather, it is an orientation point that guides a company's movement in a specific direction.

Complex metaphors can come from many places and many sources. Try out a few ideas—and think aesthetically. It's worth the time and effort to find a good metaphor to help reinforce your vision.

A Backward Glance at This Chapter

Choosing language to frame people's actions or events is like moving a telescope into position. It may, however, be only a momentary positioning until we or others communicate again to frame another reality. In this chapter, we have taken the telescope and moved it into several new positions, corresponding to five basic framing tools:

- *Metaphors* show a subject's likeness to something else and thus allow that subject to take on new meanings. The downside is that metaphors can mask important alternative meanings.
- *Jargon* and *catchphrases* frame a subject in familiar terms; however, the terms can be overused.
- *Contrast* frames a subject in terms of its opposite because it is sometimes easier to define what our subject is not rather than state what it is. In using contrast or analyzing it, note that a poor contrast can skew meaning.
- *Spin* casts the subject in a positive or negative light. When the spin-to-fact ratio becomes excessive, credibility is lost.
- *Stories* frame a subject by example and engage our attention and emotions. They are also useful teaching tools. Like metaphors, they can mask or hide meaning.
- *Complex metaphors* have many implied meanings and represent useful tools around which to build a vision. In using them, we must be careful that they not diverge too far from images that others might expect.

Mastering these tools takes time and effort but can make for impressive results. In the next chapter, we explore the consequences of combining these language tools and their effect on our behavior and the behavior of others.

Chapter Six

Avoiding Mixed Messages

The training and development manager for a large manufacturing plant in the aerospace industry was both amused and concerned when he heard the company's Total Quality Management slogan had been altered by shop floor workers. The new version: "Drive out fear (and if you can't, we'll find someone who will)." The manager had to laugh that employees, with a clever amendment to TQM's catchphrase, had created a dead-on characterization of the company's culture. But he was concerned, too, because they had neutralized the rallying cry of the initiative he hoped would change that culture.

As managers of meaning, the tools we use to frame our subjects will be but one stitch in a tapestry that we weave. As we see with the TQM catchphrase, our language tools will combine with other language and with our behavior to form meanings that perhaps we did not intend. Others may discern patterns in the tapestry that we ourselves do not see.

When the meanings we manage complement and reinforce one another, they create a clear and consistent image of our subject that helps others to know how to respond. When these meanings coalesce to reveal shading and nuance for our subject, they show that our mental models are well developed. Conversely, when the meanings we manage diverge and contradict one another, they create a fragmented view of our subject. The psychological discomfort caused by the contradictory signals often causes confusion, inertia, or behaviors opposite to those anticipated.

In this chapter, we focus on the consequences of combining language tools and the remedies we can use when the meanings we manage create mixed messages.

Warning Signals for Misunderstandings

When two or more of the meanings we manage contradict one another, a mixed message is the outcome. Because mixed messages can create misunderstanding, they are generally considered poor communication. If listeners can place greater weight on one signal over another, however, a choice between messages is made. A *Business Week* profile of Ford Motor Company's chairman, Alex Trotman, nicely demonstrates this. Trotman is the man behind Ford 2000, a globalization initiative intended to remake the world's number-two automaker. In describing his management style, *Business Week* stated, "Still while he espouses teamwork, there's no mistaking that he's the boss. After backing . . . debate, he often overrides managers with his views. 'I'm doing it anyway,' is a Trotman catchphrase" (Kerwin, 1995, p. 101). So which message are people to rely on? The usual response to mixed messages is to give more weight to the message that the speaker is less able to control and that is seen as more automatic or natural given past behavior. It's not much of a leap to imagine how Trotman's comments and behavior are interpreted.

In the following pages, we discuss the ways in which mixed messages are created using the language tools of the previous chapter. We begin first with mixed messages in metaphor usage, which presents a rather special case because of the complex meaning structure of metaphors.

Metaphors, Mixed Messages, and Entailments

In earlier examples, we have seen the value of complex metaphors, a category of metaphors that have multiple implied meanings instantly applicable to the subject of our framing. Remember the "two different faces" metaphor that was used by Pete, the team leader who couldn't show his human side to his team? This complex metaphor carries many possible meanings.

- Pete has multiple personas.
- Others' perceptions of Pete differ sharply.
- Pete reveals different parts of himself in different situations.
- Pete's surface image is not necessarily the real Pete.

In Pete and John's conversation, John used a metaphor when he suggested Pete's image was "hard core." Though "two different faces" and "hard core" are metaphors with different implied meanings, on an unconscious level we sense a fit that allows them to be used together. This fit is the result of the two metaphors having shared entailments. *Entailments* are the relationships and concepts that a metaphor brings to mind (Lakoff and Johnson, 1980). *Shared entailments* occur when the relationships and concepts of two different metaphors overlap. Even though two metaphors may highlight and hide different aspects of a subject, shared entailments suggest a sufficient coherence between them to permit and invite their combined use.

The "two different faces" and "hard core" metaphors share entailments related to surfaces and depth. For example, something that is hard to the core possesses both a surface and a center. Similarly, the notion of two faces—even the "two-faced," the "person behind the mask," or the "inner self" variations on this metaphor—suggests surface qualities versus deeper, more real personas. The shared entailments related to surfaces and depth work together to structure the meanings for Pete's behavior.

Mixed messages occur when there are no shared entailments and the meanings evoked by the metaphors actually contradict one another. The president of a large service organization supplies an excellent example. Like many organizations, his company had a history of top-down management control. Senior management played it pretty close to the vest on sharing information, especially with lower managerial ranks. As a typical example, one assistant store manager complained that he learned of his promotion to store manager from a truck driver a full twelve hours before his manager told him! An internal survey documented numerous communication problems and, not surprisingly, a highly accurate and speedy grapevine among the company's truck drivers.

After learning of these problems, the president made employee communications a goal for the year. He saw an opportunity to get the ball rolling on this new initiative when he was invited to give a speech to a meeting of the marketing regions' personnel officers.

The president spoke for about an hour and laced his speech with a number of stirring metaphors. For example, in his early remarks, the president used metaphor to portray his vision of employee communications at the company. He framed the company as an extended family and noted three things about conflict within families. First, conflict within families was both natural and valuable. Second, great ideas and solutions are often born of productive conflict. Finally, families may disagree, but they stand united against those who would harm them. Productive conflict within the "family-unit" was now to be encouraged as an opening up of communications within the company.

The president then introduced the team metaphor, stressing that everyone in the company was on the same team, united and working toward a common goal. He said that in order for the team to win, everyone must understand his or her role in making better communications a priority. The president also reflected on the process of change. He said that the company's ideal posture must be to remain "itchy and restless," to never "stand still," and to continue "growing." The president then spoke of a "journey" and the "new frontiers" that would never be discovered with complacent attitudes.

At the end of his speech, the president turned his attention to the unique role of the personnel manager in helping achieve the new communication goals in their marketing regions. At this time, he invoked one final metaphor. In referring to his communication objectives, he said, "The train is leaving. You had better not be the last ones to jump onto the train, or you will find your seat taken." The president then asked if there were any questions about the company and its new direction. Interestingly, several personnel managers had questions, but none involved any aspect of employee communications. This proved to be a telling sign.

For several of the personnel managers, the president's metaphor about missing the train became part of a running joke that lasted the duration of the three-day meeting. Their references to "missing the train" and "losing one's seat" showed that a one-minute sentence or two by the president had easily overpowered fifty-five minutes of family, team, and new frontiers framing. Several personnel managers felt that the threat implied by the metaphor of missing the train contradicted the president's goals for improved communication.

We can analyze this speech using Lakoff and Johnson's notion (1980) of entailments. To aid our analysis, we can also use John

Clancy's *The Invisible Powers* (1989), the book that analyzes the major metaphors of business in the last two centuries. Drawing from Lakoff and Johnson, Clancy analyzes the entailments of six key business metaphors—many of which are represented in the president's speech. The six metaphors and their entailments are listed in Table 6.1.

Each entailment reflects a concept or relationship that the metaphor evokes. For example, the game metaphor implies a goal, some degree of difficulty and unpredictability, fun, teamwork, and leadership. If two metaphors share entailments, we can use them together and still produce a coherent message. For example, while business-as-game and business-as-journey do not present a single, consistent image, they do share some common entailments. They both imply a goal, difficulty, unpredictability, and the need for teamwork and leadership. Thus, because the entailments implied by the metaphor are shared, they produce a coherent message.

Let's return again to the metaphors that the company president used. He invoked a family metaphor and talked about healthy conflict within families. The family metaphor is a variation of the traditional society metaphor (Table 6.1). The company president stressed the social cohesiveness of families that allows conflict to occur without disintegrating the family. The president also invoked a team metaphor, which is derivative of the game metaphor (Table 6.1). Again, though teams and families come from a different metaphorical base, they share some common entailments that allow our company president to create a coherent message. Both teams and families have a purpose or goal in common, which requires groups of people to cooperate and work interdependently to achieve the goal.

On the subject of change, the president said that the company and its people must remain itchy and restless, two metaphors that seem quite consistent with one another. If one is itchy, one is also restless, though the opposite is not necessarily true. The "itchy" and "restless" metaphors were combined with the metaphors of "never standing still" and "new frontiers." Though "itchy," "restless," and "never standing still" conjure up bodily images and the "new frontiers" conjures up a journey, these metaphors nevertheless produce a coherent message. They share the common entailment of movement.

Table 6.1. Business Metaphors and Their Entailments.

Business Metaphor	Related Term	Entailments
Journey	*Voyage*	Goal, difficulty, wealth, production, unpredictability, need for leadership, need for cooperation and teamwork
Game	*Teams*	Goals, difficulty, fun, unpredictability, teamwork, leadership
War	*Military*	Goal, difficulty, need for strong leadership, risk, strategy
Machine	*Cogs*	A wealth-producing tool, serious purpose, calculability, predictability (up to a point)
Organism	*Organic*	Complexity, ambiguity, evolution
Society	*Community*	Meaningful existence, purpose, culture, cooperation and competition, power and politics, values, leadership
	Traditional society	Social cohesiveness, immutable class structure
	Modern society	Participation, social mobility, less cohesiveness and meaning

That leaves only the "missing the train" metaphor. "Missing the train" and "losing one's seat" draws from an abandonment metaphor containing a thinly veiled threat. It contradicts what is known about the cohesiveness and inclusiveness of families and the cooperativeness and spirit of team functioning. Healthy families and teams support and cooperate with those in need of help—they do not abandon them. The quick negative reaction of the personnel managers seems to be a recognition of this fact.

In criticizing the company president's use of the "missing the train" metaphor, we are not suggesting that it never be used. We are suggesting that there are times to motivate and persuade and other times to deliver threats and warnings.

Other Language Tools and Mixed Messages

Mixed messages can be created with language tools other than metaphors. For example, we began the chapter with a mixed message that was created by a clever turn of the TQM catchphrase: "Drive out fear (and if you can't, we'll find someone who will)." We also noted the contradiction between Alex Trotman's catchphrase, "I'm doing it anyway," and his theoretical support of debate and teamwork. For another example, we return to the 1992 presidential campaign. When he was still an undeclared presidential candidate, Ross Perot spoke to the NAACP in Nashville, Tennessee. Perot was looking for votes, so it wasn't surprising that equality was the theme about which he spoke to this mostly black audience. Unfortunately, his use of language, and particularly his choice of multiple stories, did anything but sound a theme of equality.

At the beginning of Perot's speech, he told the audience that what was coming to them came straight from his heart. He spoke at length about the need for everyone to be "equal partners" and that his mother and father showed him from a very early age through their example that everyone was equal. Contradicting this message was a rhetorical question that he posed early in the speech over who is hurt first when economic times are tough. The answer he gave was "your people," an off-sounding colloquialism. Immediately, objections could be heard from the audience, but Perot could not discern the substance of the remarks. Because Perot first said "you people" and then "your people," and because "my people" is a common reference among managers, it appeared he was searching for the correct language but had momentarily stumbled. While he might have been forgiven for this transgression, he went on to tell several stories that smacked of white paternalism toward a black underclass.

He told of how his father was an employer of poor blacks, and how his dad took care of them even when they were old. He spoke of how his mother always fed black hoboes. And he spoke of having a paper route in the poorest section of town where illiteracy was high and the seeming need for newspapers was low among blacks. The lesson he reportedly learned was that the African-Americans of his childhood "were just like everybody else." Yet, he did not speak of his own history of employing African-Americans, his own business dealings with them, or any situation in which they might have been on a more equal footing in terms of social or economic power. The juxtaposition of three stories in which blacks were always the underclass and whites were always in authority and his references to "your people"— and later in the speech, to "your folks"—sent mixed signals about equality that later created a firestorm of controversy for Perot.

Thus, through our language and through the images we create with it, it is quite possible to send mixed signals and destroy the integrity of the message we hope to send.

The Messages of Behavior

Mixed messages can be produced by more than just contradictory language forms. Sometimes the meanings we have managed with our language are contradicted by our actions. In the following example, Ray is a manager who admonishes Joe, his direct report, for his use of "lay-ons" (the company's jargon for an order or direct command) with the staff. Examine how Ray responds when Joe disagrees with him:

(1) *Ray:* I have a feeling that we could implement this in a manner other than a lay-on. There have been so darn many lay-ons around here lately.

(2) *Joe:* I don't have any problems with certain lay-ons. If they're absurd, however, it's a very tough pill to swallow.

(3) *Ray:* They become a way of life after awhile.

(4) *Joe:* Yes, they can be.

(5) *Ray:* And that's not the direction that we want to go. We want to get our employees to own the business and assume more responsibility for making decisions and their own actions. That just doesn't happen when you're giving more and more and more orders about what you want done and how you want it done.

(6) *Joe:* I don't know. We could have a long conversation about this.

(7) *Ray:* Yep, we could.

(8) *Joe:* I think once we reach minimum standards of performance, there need not be any lay-ons. But if we assume that we're going to achieve these standards on a voluntary basis with this group of people, I think we're really mistaken. I think that's part of our problem. Our standards are well below what we would call minimally acceptable, and in order to get to that acceptable point, I think it is going to take some lay-ons. It's going to take some practice. It is going to take breaking old habits, and those are done in a lay-on with this group.

(9) *Ray:* Yeah, you're right. We can spend an awful lot of time talking about that that I don't think we have right now.

(10) *Joe:* Sure. Right.

Ray seems unaware of the contradictions inherent in his language and behavior. Note that Ray frames the desired goal as getting employees to "own the business" and take on more responsibility *(5)*. This "own the business" metaphor is derivative of the society metaphor (Table 6.1). The values of participation and ownership reflect change as an inherently social process of communication to achieve buy-in. Giving orders or "lay-ons" invokes military and war metaphors that effect change through domination. Though Ray effectively frames "lay-ons" as the wrong direction, his cutting off of Joe by dismissing the subject is nothing if not a "lay-on" *(9)*.

As we said earlier, when a mixed message is produced, interpretation can still be relatively easy. This conversation provides a good example. Ray's treatment of his metaphors produced a coherent message up to the point that he dismissed Joe's objections. At the point at which he blocked further discussion, Ray took on the behavior he was disavowing. What do you think Joe believes about the changeover to participative management now? Joe experiences a "lay-on" and most likely categorizes the "own the business" framing as empty rhetoric. When put to a test, Ray's actions did not back up his words.

Reading Others' Expectations

Sometimes the entailments of our language are consistent with our behavior, but they contradict the expectations of others. Often this occurs when jargon is used that is unfamiliar to some of those present. The following story by an unknown doctor, related to the authors by another person years ago, provides just such an example:

> I learned something of the intricacies of plain English at an early stage in my career. A woman of thirty-five came in one day to tell me that she wanted a baby but that she had been told that she had a certain type of heart disease which might not interfere with a normal life but would be dangerous if she ever had a baby. From her description, I thought at once of mitral stenosis. This condition is characterized by a rather distinctive rumbling murmur near the apex of the heart, and especially by a peculiar vibration felt by the examining finger on the patient's chest. The vibration is known as the "thrill" of mitral stenosis.
>
> When this woman had been undressed and was lying on my table in her white kimono, my stethoscope quickly found the heart-sounds I had expected. Dictating to my nurse, I described them carefully. I put my stethoscope aside and felt intently for the typical vibrations which may be found in a small but variable area of the left chest. I closed my eyes for better concentration. I felt long and carefully for the tremor. I did not find it and with my hand still on the woman's bare breast, lifting it upward and out of the way, I finally turned to the nurse and said, "No thrill."
>
> The patient's black eyes snapped open and with venom in her voice she said, "Well, isn't that just too bad? Perhaps it's just as well you don't get one. That isn't what I came for!" My nurse almost choked, and my explanation still seems a nightmare in futile words.

Jargon can be the source of mixed messages in almost any situation. Store managers often tell employees to "Go face the shelves." Experienced employees know they are being asked to pull products forward and make the shelves appear full, to "put on a good face." New employees wind up staring in bewilderment at the shelves, perhaps wondering why they are being punished.

As an example of another type of mixed message resulting from others' expectations, consider the autocratic plant manager who headed up a plant that had been organized since its inception with self-managing teams. Sound a little contradictory? In fact, it was not uncommon in the organization, for two reasons. First, what was seen as autocratic from below was often seen as decisive and direction setting from above. Second, team-based or "technician" systems were often regarded as relating primarily to the lower ranks of plant personnel. In this particular plant, however, there were teams throughout the plant hierarchy, including a plant manager work team.

When we first visited the plant on a consulting assignment, we were taken out to dinner by the plant manager and his work team. We found it odd, however, that during the dinner the plant manager acted like a traffic cop in dominating the flow of the conversation. Like school children, the members of his team, all high-ranking managers in the plant, seemed to speak only when spoken to. When they spoke, their communication was superficially polite and perfunctory. It was not until we listened to tape recordings of the plant manager's daily interactions with his staff that our dinner conversation began to make some sense (Basden, 1991). Laced throughout the plant manager's conversations with his team were the following military and war metaphors:

Salute it	Reinforcements
Strategic choices	Support
Tactical choices	Rank
Attacking aggressively	Betraying
Service to the fleet	March toward
Come front and center	Capture, recapture
Fire away	Assignment
Rally around	Confront
Get them in the boat	Taking it over
Bail out	Join up with
Coming from behind	Terminate
Withdrawal	

The language and behavior of this plant were supposed to reflect the combined societal and team metaphors of Table 6.1. *Self-management* reflected the societal aspect, which emphasizes ownership and participation. The team metaphor stressed interdependence, shared responsibility, and cooperation. In the hands of this military-minded plant manager, however, the system developed its own mutations. The teams were in place, yet they functioned like hierarchies. Participation was said to be valued, yet the reality was top-down direction and communication. Process was supposed to matter, yet it was lip service to the focus on winning by whatever means. The plant manager's military metaphors produced a coherent set of signals insofar as his actions were concerned. The mixed message came from the expectations of him created by the company and the history and design of the factory. Company proclamations of participative systems and new age empowerment philosophies notwithstanding, the language of war and the military produced a culture that only Patton would have loved.

Become a Detective: Investigate Mixed Messages

In order to be more aware of our mixed messages, we must look for clues that indicate how our meanings play out. AT&T did this on an organizational level with its "archetype studies." Like many other companies during the eighties, AT&T became enamored of Japanese management ideas while ignoring the cultural factors that might make ideas work in some cultural contexts but not in others (Bowles and Hammond, 1991).

Marilyn Zuckerman, AT&T's manager of quality planning, was one of the managers who commissioned an innovative set of studies whose mission was "to understand how quality is perceived in America so that we could create a model that could work for Americans, both at home and in the workplace" (Bowles and Hammond, 1991, p. 169).

AT&T hired a consultant, G. Clotaire Rapaille, a French-born psychologist and marketing expert who specialized in "archetype studies." Rapaille's belief, based on Jungian and Gestalt theory, was that members of a culture have imprinted mental codes—archetypes—that are structures providing permanent meaning. In his studies, Rapaille sought to discover deep-seated cultural meanings.

For ten months during 1986, AT&T sought to find the archetype for quality. They used focus groups in which participants were asked to move beyond simple opinions to recall their "first, most important, and most recent" experiences with quality. As they discussed these experiences, cultural meanings for quality were revealed—with surprising results. AT&T researchers discovered two distinctively American characteristics associated with quality that called into question the wholesale transplantation of Japanese management ideas. The first was both strongly emotional and negative, related to a recurrent theme of not being able to meet the expectations of others. Bowles and Hammond (1991) who report of this effort, note that if Americans associate quality with feelings of inadequacy, it is little wonder that the quality directives "do it right the first time," "zero defects," and "the customer is always right," evoke a less than positive response. Seen in the context of the American archetype for quality, these phrases create mixed messages.

The second theme was that quality is equated with "it works," whereas perfection connotes "the end," or "the job is finished." This notion runs contrary to TQM's "continuous improvement," suggesting another weak spot in the wholesale adoption of TQM.

AT&T's archetype studies illuminated not only places where themes and vocabularies might create mixed messages but where visions and programs need bolstering with new concepts and language. AT&T devised a change program and, using the archetype focus groups, tested the words it would use, which included *impossible dream, lawgiver, crisis, mentor, coach, celebration,* and *champion.* The company then could actively manage the new meanings of these terms. Here is an example: "Out go the traditional meanings. The impossible dream has a serious role in business. . . . Mentors in the archetype definition don't help you on your way through the system but are there to identify with your emotions when things go wrong; coaches at work, like real coaches, help you practice your skills, and they are there when it's your turn to bat again— they are not left in the corporate training rooms with the textbooks and process" (Bowles and Hammond, 1991, p. 170).

Managing new meanings for mentor and coach should significantly alter the role of the traditional manager. The archetype studies are really an attempt to understand deeply held meanings and avert mixed messages in the cross-cultural transplantation of management ideas or in the formulation of management initiatives.

Archetype studies might have prevented the adoption and subsequent rejection of Japanese quality circles in many U.S. companies in the 1980s. In quality circles, the leader is still very much in charge of team functioning, thus maintaining the organization's hierarchy despite the implied meanings of the circle metaphor. Moreover, members tend only to make suggestions with little or no decision-making power (Nishiyama, 1981). These qualities fit well within the Japanese culture, which emphasizes deference to authority; they do not fit very well in the more independence-minded United States.

Self-managing team-based systems, in which leadership shifts to the most knowledgeable party and the job of the manager is to get the team to lead itself, have proven successful in many American companies. Thus, if there had been an understanding that Japanese teams tend toward hierarchy and that U.S. teams would tend toward autonomy, costly experiments with U.S. quality circles and confusion over decision making within teams might have been avoided (Fairhurst and Wendt, 1993).

Obviously, each of us, as individuals or even as distinct companies, cannot perform archetype studies. But if we have the opportunity to plan our framing attempts ahead of time, we can think through and possibly discuss with colleagues how our framing and actions fit within a wider context. Look for clues and gut-level intuitions that indicate some incongruence, that something is not right. Then examine how a subject might be reframed and compare that alternative framing with the first.

When we do not have time to examine beforehand the implications of our framing, then we should be especially careful to examine any mixed messages after the fact. Did something go wrong? Were we criticized for a mixed signal? Was it justified? These are just a few of the questions to pose. With practice, asking questions—and knowing the right questions to ask—can become second nature.

Unmixing the Message

We may wish that the world were a simpler place to live in. But the fact is that paradox and contradiction surround us. If our language use contradicts other communications, our own actions, or others' expectations, we can choose to deal directly with these contradictions and the attendant mixed messages by communicating about them and making them the subject of our framing. By treating the mixed message as a subject for framing, we create opportunities to influence its interpretation.

Through reframing, we can affect the interpretation of the mixed message in three ways:

1. We can acknowledge that there is indeed a contradiction and that the contradiction must be understood for all of its ramifications.
2. We can show how the contradiction is more apparent than real. We can, in some way, show that the signals are really consistent with one another.
3. We can change our language to realign it with other things we have said, with our actions, or with others' expectations.

With these last two actions, we "unmix" the mixed signals.

Recall the service chain example earlier in the chapter? After the company president delivered the speech, we sent him a memo. We described the negative reactions of the personnel managers and their displeasure over the implied threat. The president responded by acknowledging the contradiction in his message and by framing this case as "an exception."

> I appreciate both the spirit and candor surrounding your message to me. The observation you made concerning the distinction between persuasion and coercion is not one with which I disagree, generally. This time, however, the circumstances presented an exception.
>
> The personnel managers for a long time have been challenged to exert leadership in the employee communications area. They have not met that challenge, unfortunately. For that reason, I wanted them to know that this was not just another appeal. It was, clearly, a change in their job content and a sharpening of our expectations of them as individuals.
>
> The train reference is familiar to that group, since it was used by one of their peers for many years. And, like you, I believe they got the message. At the same time, you know that their response to date has been anything but impressive. They still need to be pushed and cajoled.
>
> A harsh judgment? Perhaps. A fair judgment? I certainly believe so. Again, I appreciate your comments and do not find

myself in disagreement with them. I simply considered that meeting as an exception to the general rule of persuade and sell rather than mandate and tell.

The president clearly intended to both persuade and mandate, realizing that "mandate" would be the more powerful message. Could the president have altered his communication to deliver his message with better effect? Could he have communicated about the mixed message more directly to the personnel managers? We think so, and we believe that it would have been a communication with a more positive impact.

A Backward Glance at This Chapter

One way to ruin an otherwise good attempt at framing is to mix the messages, to send contradictory signals. This chapter discussed how we can be more alert to the pitfalls of mixed messages and how we can alleviate the damage they cause. To this end, here are some specific guidelines.

- Mixed messages involve contradictions between our words and our other communications and behavior or between our words and others' expectations.
- Interpretation of the mixed signal will usually depend upon which of the signals is perceived to be more genuine.
- Contradictions between metaphors can be resolved by considering their *entailments*—the concepts and relationships that they bring to mind.
- When mixed messages occur by oversight or because they are unavoidable, treat the mixed signals as the subject for framing. A contradiction can be more thoroughly described and its interpretation thus influenced in a positive way.

Since most of our communications are spontaneous and do not give us time to prepare before we speak, how do we avoid the pitfalls of mixed messages and improve our ability to frame spontaneously? The next chapter will answer this question by explaining how to prime for spontaneity.

Chapter Seven

Preparing Yourself to Frame Spontaneously

Gifted communicators make it all look so simple. Words just seem to slip off their tongues with ease. Whether it is the educated style of William Buckley or Barbara Jordan, the plain-spokenness of Lee Iacocca, the oratory of Jesse Jackson, the enthusiastic delivery of Tom Peters, or the storytelling ability of Frederick Crawford, we admire these people's way with words. Because so much of our communication demands spontaneity, it's easy to think that gifted communicators were born with talents that others do not share. With little apparent effort, they seem automatically and unconsciously to choose just the right words to say.

This admiration for gifted communicators and acknowledgment that many communications are spontaneous and automatic raises the question of how effective the rest of us can be at framing. If we unconsciously select our words, of what use are framing tools? How can we take the time to be concerned about preventing mixed messages? Can we learn to communicate our vision spontaneously, or must we be born with the talent? Can we exert control over a process that is seemingly spontaneous? How much is it possible to change our current communications, and where do we begin?

The answers may surprise you. The idea of controlling spontaneity may seem paradoxical, but it can be done through priming. This chapter will show you why you should prime for spontaneity—and how to do it.

Goals and Spontaneity: Merging the Two

Pick up any self-help book or recall the last seminar on communications that you attended. Very likely, a number of assumptions were made:

- Most of what we know about our communication has been consciously learned.
- Most of our communications or, at least, most of our important communications, are planned in advance.
- We consciously carry out our advance plans when we communicate.

While there are several situations for which these assumptions hold, these are incorrect assumptions for the majority of communication situations in which we find ourselves. The fact is that most of our communications, including a great many of our most important communications, occur without much preparation and without much awareness of how we select and arrange the words we use.

In both spontaneous and planned communications, we communicate when we have a point to make or a feeling to convey; in other words, when we have a goal. Can we be strategic and goal oriented and at the same time be spontaneous and automatic? Actually, this question is not as contradictory as it sounds. As the discussion of emergent goals in Chapter Two revealed, communicating spontaneously means that we are still conscious of having a goal or certain ideas in mind. It's just that our emergent goals are not preplanned; they are established as we work toward other, planned goals.

Becoming conscious of a goal purposely but unconsciously predisposes us to manage meaning in one direction or another to communicate our frames (Kellerman, 1992). We may be conscious of a goal (without this consciousness, we couldn't work a conversation around a specific topic) but unconscious of how we will select, structure, and exchange words with another person to achieve that goal. Our unconscious mind makes certain communication options available to us for the framing that we ultimately do. These options are not always ones we would have consciously chosen, as we are painfully aware when we blunder and succumb to "foot-in-mouth" disease. But we can increase our chances of selecting an appropriate and effective option: we can "program" our unconscious toward the selection of certain options over others via priming. When we use the process of priming, we call to mind our mental models, anticipated opportunities, and/or desirable language sometime prior to communicating. As the following discussion reveals, the key to controlling spontaneous communication lies not in something we consciously do at the time of communication but in our primed memories.

Preparing and Priming Mental Models

In the movie *Field of Dreams,* starring Kevin Costner, an Iowa farmer hears voices that tell him to build a baseball diamond right in the middle of his cornfield. This was an odd bit of advice for a farmer in serious financial trouble, but the voice persisted. "If you build it, he will come," the voice whispered. The farmer came to believe that he was to build the field for Shoeless Joe Jackson, a baseball player banned from the game after being accused of throwing the 1919 World Series between the Chicago White Sox and the Cincinnati Reds. Jackson was also the idol of the farmer's deceased father, from whom the farmer had been estranged at the time the father died. After the farmer built the field, Shoeless Joe Jackson did indeed appear, and with him came the other seven banned White Sox players. Eventually, many other players of long ago who had dreamed of playing again came to the "field of dreams." This included the farmer's father, who had been a minor-league ballplayer. When the farmer saw his father, he realized that he had built the field as much for the realization of his own dream of reconciling with his dad as for the dreams of Joe Jackson and the other players.

With slight variation, the whispered command, "If you build it, he will come," holds the answer to the question, "How do we get better at framing our spontaneous and automatic communications?" We need a way to construct not a baseball diamond but mental models. We need to build mental models from which our communications can flow; the phrase "if you build them, they will come" can help remind us of that. Then, having developed mental models, we can periodically bring them into our conscious awareness by simple reflection or by communicating about them to others. Each time we bring our mental models to the surface in these ways, we prime our unconscious to use them in spontaneous communication. If you prime your mental models, frames will come.

To understand this better, we turn to the work of several psychologists who study cognition and memory. Psychologist John Bargh argues that we are consciously aware of only a subset of what is contained in our memories (Bargh, 1989). For example, have you ever been asked a question and had the distinct feeling of knowing an answer, yet you couldn't produce that answer? While you stammer silently, someone else answers the question, and you say to yourself, "I knew that!" In such instances, something about the activation of your memory gives you the feeling of knowing— even while you have no conscious awareness of the answer.

Bargh and other psychologists say that when we become conscious of a goal, many conscious and unconscious sources of information that influence our judgment and behavior are triggered in our memories. One source of information occurs when some recent experience or thinking exercise that we are fully aware of influences information that we later absorb and interpret in ways we are quite unaware of. The exercise of consciously thinking about a subject "primes" our unconscious mind to see and interpret subsequent information in ways consistent with our earlier thinking.

In laboratory experiments, psychologists demonstrate this effect by activating a social construct in one context and finding that the people in the experiments then use that construct to interpret the behavior of a target person in a second and completely unrelated context (Bargh, 1989). For example, if the construct is hostility, then the subjects in the experiment use hostility to interpret the other, unrelated situation. Priming also occurs in "tip-of-the-tongue" situations when a word that we cannot remember comes to mind later in an unrelated conversation or activity. The conscious experience of wanting to remember the word primes the unconscious to search for that word even after the goal of remembering leaves our conscious mind. (A similar situation occurs when we think of the perfect comeback in the shower.)

If a particular thought process was a part of one's recent conscious experience, then that thought process remains accessible and used by the unconscious mind to filter information taken in later. This occurs for some time after that thought process is no longer in one's conscious awareness. It's a little like putting on your sunglasses on a sunny day: you have the initial experience of less glare, but you quickly forget that you are seeing with a colored lens. So too with priming our unconscious mind. Our conscious experience has dissolved but has primed our unconscious with a lens that influences our view, though we are quite unaware of its presence. The more frequently we prime, the more permanent the lens that influences our seeing (Fiske and Taylor, 1991).

This carries significant implications for the control of our framing when we spontaneously communicate. If we take the time to consciously and periodically think through our mental models (answering such questions as, "What are our models about? What assumptions do they rely on?"), we are priming our unconscious to select and interpret new information using the models as a reference point. Our models become consciously chosen as the unconscious lenses for seeing and interpreting the environment around us and framing it for others.

We prime, however, not just by reflecting upon our mental models but also by communicating them. An awareness of what we say when we communicate our mental models to others primes the unconscious in the same way that reflecting on them does. Whether it is reflection or communication that brings our mental models to the surface, conscious recall leaves an unconscious imprint. That is the essence of priming. The stronger or clearer the imprint, the more our communications draw from the state of mental readiness that priming creates.

It is worth reiterating that the farmer's efforts in *Field of Dreams* turned out not to be solely for Shoeless Joe and the other players but also for his dream of reconciling with his father. It was a goal the farmer was not conscious of when he began the baseball field but one he quickly embraced at the sight of his father. It is the same way when we communicate; there will be times when it is impossible to predict how our priming will end up in actual conversation, because events and our communication partners are not always predictable. Yet our priming will be recognizable.

Priming provides a rich resource for those of us who worry

about our ability to spontaneously communicate our vision. Take the time to develop a mental model for the future. Clarify the values and mission that are the basis for this future. If you continuously develop your models for these governing ideas, you will be ready to frame for others, and your framing will be powerful.

Priming for Opportunities

How is priming different than rehearsal for a speech or some other event that demands advance planning? This is an important question. To answer it, we must first acknowledge that there are three types of situations for which we prime: specific situations, total surprises, and repeatable contexts. We will examine these situations and their priming needs in the next sections.

Specific Situations

Often we can plan for specific communication events in advance. Possible events include a speech, a performance feedback session with a difficult employee, a sales pitch to higher-ups, or a job interview with a top candidate. Priming in these situations is the same as rehearsal. We anticipate a specific context and audience and choose our goals and communication strategies ahead of time. We check the fit of our mental models with our communication goals, and we make sure we are being sensitive to the context in which we will be communicating. Finally, we consciously select the best framing tools for conveying our message.

Total Surprises

There are also situations that are totally unanticipated. In these situations, we envision neither a specific nor a typical context. A friend of the authors recently came face to face with a total surprise when her boss informed her that he was leaving his wife of twenty-five years and his four children for a homosexual lover. Apparently, he had privately struggled with his sexual identity for some time and had only recently accepted his homosexuality. He was letting his employee know because he felt that the turmoil in his life was influencing his job performance.

The employee was initially speechless when she heard this totally unexpected news. Her response, when speech returned, was to draw from her own values to indicate her concern for her boss and the obvious pain he was in, her respect for whatever decision he would make, and her appreciation for his letting her know the truth of the situation. She said afterward that she had been not at all prepared for what she heard. But her response to her boss made it clear to us that, on a certain level, she had been prepared. How so? Periodically, she attends retreats at her church and clarifies her values by asking herself, "What kind of person am I? What do I stand for?" Though she may not have felt prepared for the instance she reported, by having clarified her values on a regular basis, she had prepared herself for surprises.

The most reasonable preparation we can have for the totally unexpected is to do much as this individual did and periodically prime the mental models that underlie and define our values.

Repeatable Contexts

Perhaps the greatest impact that we can have through priming is in taking advantage of repeatable contexts. Most of the work contexts in which we find ourselves do tend to repeat themselves. Whether these contexts are staff meetings, interviews, briefings, one-to-ones, or sales pitches, there is clearly a routine, a repeating pattern, to much of what we do. Unfortunately, behavior that is routine quickly turns into habit, and habit quickly turns into mindless, automatic behavior. We can make full use of the power of priming by refusing to take repeatable contexts for granted and by insisting on using them spontaneously to make our points and put forth our message.

Improvisational comedians who interact with the audience as part of their act are not as fully spontaneous as they may appear: they have previously primed much of their off-the-cuff banter, preparing for spontaneity by anticipating the common features of the audience and context and building routines around them. This, then, primes the material for use when the context presents itself. For example, comedians who tour the country's local comedy clubs often ask club owners and employees to supply them with local references to use in their stock jokes and routines about, say, the neighborhood nobody wants to be from ("Oh, you must be from . . ."), the local politician with loose morals, or the latest in local professional sports. Comedians also have primed comebacks for dealing with hecklers, usually to humiliate them into silence. While the order of the material for a comedian's performance may be quite spontaneous, much of the material itself is not because it has been primed.

In the same way that improvisational comedians prime for spontaneity, you can anticipate your repeatable contexts. Rather than plan for a specific encounter, try to visualize how your vision, for example, might play out in several typical situations: staff meetings, performance appraisals, weekly briefings, and job interviews. Imagine what your task, relational, and identity communication goals might be in each case. Then resist impulsive language use in these situations by thoughtfully considering specific subjects for your framing and the framing tools at your disposal to manage the meaning of those subjects. Go one step further and develop a useful complex metaphor.

The following story is a good example of priming for a repeatable context. Steve is a manager who is helping Brad, his direct report, prepare for several meetings with the various teams on his shift. The meetings are intended to facilitate their use of statistical process control procedures in Deming's TQM approach and to encourage people to use statistical techniques to monitor and analyze problems. In the conversation, Steve envisions several typical scenarios Brad might encounter.

Speaker	Dialogue	Explanation
Steve	*Okay, you've got these team meetings coming up— multiple meetings with the different product teams, all at different points in the process of adoption of the statistical methods. You need a starter for your meetings. Here it is. Simple terms. Everyone's role is essentially to improve quality and reduce cost.*	Steve anticipates a repeatable context. Recommends a starter for the meeting.

Speaker	Dialogue	Explanation
	The big question is, "Why is that and how does it fit?" The answer is simple. What we're trying to do is ultimately meet a customer's need. Now how I meet that need is working on things in these areas: X, Y, and Z. Fill in the blanks, of course.	
	Then you've got to create a role model, take a person in the room and say, "Okay, here's your basic role and responsibilities." Now go back in and fill in the details for that person. What you want to say is, "Okay, here's where you fit into the big picture."	Recommends creating a role model.
	So you're going through the process two times. One without much detail, and then you go to the role model. You've got some specific projects out there that the team is working on. Give some thought to what result you're expecting on the projects and how that project is going to make a difference.	Recommends using specific projects as examples.
	For example, take the folding wheel. You could say, "What I expect to do here is reduce the percentage of scrap."	
Brad	*I've got this $27 million figure somewhere. But that would be good because it reduced scrap by 80 percent.*	
Steve	*Good.*	

In this conversation, Steve and Brad are not anticipating a specific meeting but a typical one. The repeatable context is the series of meetings about statistical process methods that Brad will hold with the work teams. Steve also holds two communication goals raised in Chapter Three, namely to explain and personalize TQM ideas.

Steve adopts a kind of "plug-in" strategy when discussing a starter for the meeting, role models, and projects. He provides the structure for the general situation but leaves the specifics for Brad to fill in. Steve is anticipating the typical situation, formulating goals, and suggesting framing strategies that can be drawn upon as the situation presents itself. Steve is helping Brad to prime for spontaneity, just as you can help yourself—and help others.

Priming for High-Impact Opportunities

Within the myriad combinations of factors that merge to form the gestalt we call a context, what is it that skilled framers see and do when they read a context? All other things being equal (such as the amount of information that they possess about a subject), average framers and skilled framers often have the same instincts about a subject. Average and skilled framers differ not so much in their internal responses to a given situation as in their external responses. They both have expectations disproven, and they both experience that "something's amiss." They differ, however, in that skilled framers associate their instinctual "something's amiss" feeling with a framing opportunity—an opportunity to break into the action and influence its course. Simply put, skilled framers make maximum use of high-impact opportunities; they act on their instincts and seize the moment.

Instinct for Impact

How can we learn to use high-impact opportunities well, to prime for them ahead of time? The first step is learning more about them in general. The content of many, many everyday work conversations demonstrates that high-impact opportunities occur when

- There is unnecessary complexity.
- There is misleading information.

- There are loose ends or apparent discontinuities.
- Information is suppressed.
- Barriers to action exist.

The complexity, discontinuity, or misinformation about a subject is often readily apparent. As we become familiar with a subject, we set up expectations for how the subject should behave or how we should behave with respect to the subject. When our expectations go unconfirmed, we have an instinctual reaction that something is amiss. Sometimes we can pinpoint the problem immediately and sometimes we can't; the feeling is there in either case. How, then, do we learn to act, and to act effectively, on these instincts?

To address this issue, let's examine just what your instincts might tell you and the specific kinds of framing opportunities they present for average and skilled framers alike. As we will see, if an issue is unnecessarily complex, skilled framers simplify. If there is misleading or suppressed information, they set the record straight. If there are apparent discontinuities, they forge linkages. If barriers to action exist, they find new angles for removing them.

Problem: Unnecessary Complexity
Framing Opportunity: Get to the Heart of the Matter

Get to the Heart of the Matter

Often, we find ourselves in discussions where there is too much detail, complexity, or information. Perhaps an issue is complex or many sided. Maybe the discussion has too many digressions. Maybe our attention is being diverted from the real issue. Our instincts tell us that we are off course, lacking in the right focus. As a result, we feel overloaded with complexity or information, and we need to sort through it all.

The solution to the problem of unnecessary complexity, getting to the heart of the matter, is a framing opportunity that involves

- Breaking a complex topic into simpler parts
- Framing arguments as strong versus weak
- Framing information as key as opposed to "nice to know" or irrelevant
- Keeping focused on one's communication goals

To help make this clear, here are two examples related to getting to the heart of the matter. Chris had worked for Ed for less than a year when Ed suggested that they have a "one-to-one" to talk about how things were going between them. Ed told Chris to prepare to talk both about the things that he liked in the relationship and the things he wanted to change. Here is part of that conversation:

Chris: You know, you target in on things real well, and you don't
get involved in a lot of the fluff.

Ed: [*Laughs.*]

Chris: When you target, you just go right to the meat of the problem. That's been real good for me. You've really opened
up some problems that have never really been opened up.

Ed: Can you give me any examples of that?

Chris: The way you openly worked the staffing issue. The way you
have admitted the criteria problems that we have and how
we've administered those criteria. We have never had a
group manager that would admit things like that.

Ed: Really?

Chris: The way you have identified the problem that we have
with the mill population. We have technicians between
five and fourteen years that we have a significant problem
with, and no group manager has targeted the problem
like you have. So that kind of analysis has been excellent.

Ed recognizes that framing the essence or "meat" of a problem is a framing opportunity that should not be passed up. His framing and analysis of problems also appears to have made Chris feel more empowered.

Consider the next conversation between Janice, a department manager, and Lucy, her direct report. They are talking about suggesting some rather aggressive goals for Lucy's team, which comprises many older men. Examine how Janice gets to the heart of the matter with her framing of the real issue behind Lucy's statements:

Lucy: I'm just not sure we should go forward with such an
aggressive plan. I mean, there are so many things to consider. We found out the other day that the absenteeism

for B team for February was the highest in three years.
We've got the technology change coming down soon,
and we have no idea what that's going to bring. And you
know Daniels will not be silent on that one.

Janice: Lucy, there is no question in my mind that we might be
living with Murphy's Law on this one. But I think the
real issue is your not wanting to confront Daniels on this.
This guy is going to challenge you on these goals, and
you don't want to take him on. I can understand that,
but I think you have to ask yourself, "What's best for this
team right now? Also, what's best for Lucy Peters in the
long run?"

In this conversation, Janice can see through the complexities
of the situation as Lucy represents them and frames "the real issue"
as Janice sees it. Lucy's choice is to agree or disagree with Janice.
But if she agrees (and the ensuing discussion showed that she did),
then Janice's framing facilitates good problem solving because it
keeps them from wasting time on superfluous issues.

> *Problem:* Misleading Information
> *Framing Opportunity:* Correct the Sleight of Hand

Correct the Sleight of Hand

The more information that we have about a subject, the more we
are able to take apart arguments and spot what is false, misleading,
or illusory. Our instincts usually don't fail us on this one. We often
feel a strong impulse to be negative toward fallacious reasoning or
stereotyped thinking. This framing opportunity merely exposes the
fallacies and/or reveals the myths.

A good example of correcting the sleight of hand was provided
by Rosabeth Moss Kanter in her 1977 book *Men and Women of the
Corporation.* During the decade of the 1970s, women were beginning to come into the workforce in large numbers, and there was
much discussion and debate about the female stereotype. The
stereotype was that women wouldn't make good managers because
they were overly jealous, emotional, petty, critical, too detail oriented, and not "businesslike" because they would take things too
personally.

Kanter's framing of the issue, however, turned this stereotype on its head. Kanter examined women's behavior in the context of all powerless people in the organization. On the subject of women's supposed bossiness she wrote: "Stereotypes persist even in the face of evidence negating them. The real extent of bossiness among women in authority in organizations may have little to do with the persistence of the stereotype, but this particular portrait has one very important characteristic: *It is a perfect picture of people who are powerless. Powerlessness tends to produce those very characteristics attributed to women bosses.* A careful look at comparisons between men and women supposedly in the same position shows that what looks like sex differences may really be power differences" (p. 202, emphasis added).

Kanter does a masterful job of reframing the context through which women are seen. Bossiness is not framed as "femaleness" but as powerlessness, and so she corrects a sleight of hand that had been used for many years to keep women from advancing in the organization. Kanter's statement demonstrates that correcting a sleight of hand, when done well, can deliver a real punch because something that is taken for granted or cleverly masked is suddenly revealed for what it is. In another example of this, pay close attention to what Bill says in the following conversation:

Sue: And I had requested him to write up a draft of the letter, basically stating that we can meet production requirements for test market, but we'll have higher-than-normal scrap rates. He's going to do a draft and run that by you.
Bill: Good weasel words.
Sue: Aren't they?
Bill: Higher-than-normal scrap rates?
Sue: Higher than normal, I know. Somebody would love to say, "Well, what does that mean exactly?"

When Bill reveals Sue's sleight of hand, it comes as almost a surprise because the words Sue has chosen, "higher-than-normal scrap rates," seem ambiguous and innocuous at the same time. "Good weasel words" delivers an immediate punch by unmasking Sue's deliberate attempt to be ambiguous.

Another route to correcting the sleight of hand is to reveal fallacious reasoning for what it is. There are many, many ways to distort an argument with faulty reasoning, such as oversimplifying, drawing hasty conclusions, begging the question, and circular reasoning. Identifying faulty reasoning is a major step toward eliminating its use in the context of an argument. A good example is found in a conversation between a team manager, Harold, and his direct report, "Jonesy." They are talking about the need to bring certain of the team members up to minimum skill levels.

(1) *Harold:* The lines have so far not been able to get their efficiencies back. Like Line One, even if it bogs down in Birmingham, they need to get out of the doldrums and get back on the right road. Look what Jensen is able to do on Lines Eight and Nine. That's what the difference is!

(2) *Jonesy:* I wonder if Jensen can take any of that back to Line One and make it happen?

(3) *Harold:* Well, I'm not sure you can make chicken salad out of chicken s__t [*laughs*].

(4) *Jonesy:* [*Laughs.*] Well, now wait a minute. That's maybe going a little too far. Lockhart, Eckert, and Smitty— I worked with those guys, and they can be taught when it's presented right.

In this example, we see Harold's use of exaggeration with a clever put down *(3)*. After acknowledging the humorous turn of a phrase, Jonesy calls him on this strategy and names the individuals for whom this frame was an exaggeration *(4)*.

One framing strategy that may guard against the sleight of hand is to offer multiple and competing frames or interpretations of a subject. The presence of multiple plausible interpretations should give the communicators pause and encourage caution in accepting one interpretation without further information or consideration. In the following case, Carl, the plant manager, and Sue, his group manager, are talking about John, the division manager. When John visited Carl's plant, he made a passing remark to Carl during a plant walk-through that "managerial changes should be in the works." Before Carl is able to question John, he and Sue have the following conversation. Carl, especially, is trying to get to the real meaning behind this statement—and guards against a sleight of hand in the process.

Sue: You know, does it mean that we're really not sure about the Dianes of the world, so let's test them out of here? That's what I think it means. It's a signal to tighten up on our selection process.

Carl: Or, does it mean this plant has too many group managers? Does it mean that the division has too many group managers? Or does it mean that John's got some answer about the right number? I think there's a lot of ways that remark could be interpreted. But I think John is trying to do his best.

Sue: Right.

Carl: If he sees something that doesn't make sense, he'll speak out. I see John again in a half-hour, and I'll be sure to ask him.

By offering multiple plausible interpretations, the chances of settling on one interpretation, especially an incorrect one, seem lessened. This is an especially wise strategy to use at this point because so little information is available about what the division manager really meant.

Problem: Apparent Discontinuities
Framing Opportunity: Make Linkages

Make Linkages

By answering the "why" and "so what" questions others often have, we can help them resolve the discontinuities they perceive in their work environments. This is a framing opportunity that recognizes our human need to understand, to make sense of the sometimes complex and confusing circumstances we all face. If links cannot be forged between what people do and why they do it, the consequences are significant. Inertia may set in because people don't understand what they're doing. And without understanding, people are less likely to own the work.

Logically, in order to make linkages for other people, we have to know the following: What do they know? What is their purpose? What is familiar? What frames do they currently hold? Where is the space for new thinking? We must therefore be very sensitive to those with whom we speak.

The following shop floor example demonstrates a question often heard in organizations: "How does this apply to me?" Jon is Sal's team leader, and he is explaining the relevance of Total Quality Management for Sal's current task assignment:

(1) *Sal:* I see what you are saying. But I don't know if I can use that type of thing [TQM] on this current project.
(2) *Jon:* What we're really trying to do is to reach some result. And really what we wanna do is focus on this customer need. Now in your job that's the kind of things you're doing. Ultimately, you're trying to focus on the customer need. Now thinking about the consumer feedback survey that you're working on—what you're doing there is trying to understand the consumer need, okay? If you think about it, you're working on a project that affects quality and cost, where quality and cost is in the eye of the beholder, the customer, okay? If we make them more satisfied, it's likely we'll have more people buying our product.
(3) *Sal:* Okay, I think I see what you're saying.

Sal was unable to make the link between TQM and what he does. In response, Jon personalizes the TQM vision for Sal by making very specific applications to Sal's consumer feedback survey *(2)*. This enables Sal to see the relevance of TQM principles to his job. As we discussed in Chapter Three, this is the kind of framing opportunity that is essential to the implementation of a vision or program.

> *Problem:* Suppressed Information
> *Framing Opportunity:* Discover the Missing Puzzle Piece

Discover the Missing Puzzle Piece

If you take the time to analyze routine work conversation, as shown here, you discover that people make arguments in most of their interactions. Often, these arguments are based on hidden premises or assumptions or upon undrawn conclusions: something is missing, some piece of information is being suppressed. Really great framers create an opportunity from this and read between the lines, framing what has not been said. They have a knack for completing arguments by framing suppressed premises and conclusions as in, "The assumption that you are making . . . ," or, "You would have to conclude, then . . . ," or, "Your premise is. . . ."

As a result, framing to help people discover the missing puzzle piece helps them to feel as though they better understand their world. Revealing the complete arguments that someone is making often results in a more constructive debate of the issues. Exceptional framers know that not everyone accepts the premises of an argument, draws the same conclusion, or is even aware that a specific conclusion could be drawn. Because of their knowledge, exceptional framers take efforts to promote a healthier discussion by making arguments more complete.

In the following conversation, Lou, a manager, is talking to Matt, who is his direct report. Lou is giving Matt some feedback about the lack of real participation in Matt's team meetings, which he leads. As you read the conversation, see if you can determine the premises that underlie Lou's arguments.

(1) *Lou:* So, if I could somehow hold a mirror up to your average team meeting, okay? Your average team meeting for the brand is nonparticipative, non–buy-in, and not communicating openly. You are much more polite and respectful, to a certain extent, and respectful of the environment. But you are not a group of people that are truly aiming for how to make each one of us be the best that we can be or even understanding what that is for somebody, okay? There's not healthy, respectful, constructive discussion and debate. It appears to be more positioning. And that's just 'cause that's where the group is right now. That's not an indictment of anybody.

(2) *Matt:* I think the analysis is correct. If I was to do anything to get the group beyond the polite stage, I would try to be as open as I can. Not only in what I share about myself but in what I wonder about and question for understanding from the group. I want to understand what they're saying as opposed to making some judgment and then following up with a statement or a simple

question. In a nutshell, for me it's truly participating. And truly participating is not necessarily me sharing my views. It is also to understand other views and subsequently to value the diversity of that view.

(3) *Lou:* That would be a good set of principles to embrace.

(4) *Matt:* If I could say one more thing about this—the lack of disagreement doesn't always mean that people are positioning necessarily.

(5) *Lou:* No, no I agree. But the two meetings I observed, it clearly was.

The premises that underlie Lou's arguments are never voiced but had been previously supplied by the organization when it reorganized to self-managing teams and embraced Deming's TQM. Both of these interventions embrace participative management and value diversity. These premises (drawn from written documents) are as follows:

- The organization encourages free and spirited collaboration in decision making through teams.
- Work groups are responsible for all operating decisions.
- The organization will employ and promote the best people it can find without regard to race or gender or any other differences unrelated to performance. The organization will value diversity.

When Lou, the leader, frames team processes as "nonparticipative" and "more positioning," the conclusion that this must be changed is an obvious one based on the unspoken premise that participation is to be valued *(1)*.

Premises do not always have to be verbalized, because they are assumed and are part of the context. To the degree the organization has a well-developed internal campaign to inculcate key beliefs among its members, few problems in interpretation will result from suppressing key premises (Fairhurst, 1993; Tompkins and Cheney, 1985).

Matt, however, verbalizes his and the organization's premises with respect to free and spirited collaboration in decision making through teams *(2)*. He makes known the premise that participation is a two-way exchange and a valuing of the other's right to participate regardless of the content. By framing this heretofore unspoken premise, Matt defines "truly participating," and so distinguishes one set of preferred behaviors over another. When Lou endorses Matt's distinction, it reinforces their shared values *(3)*. Over the long term, these are exactly the kinds of exchanges that make people feel that they are in sync with one another and share a common value base.

Matt goes even further, however, in drawing a conclusion from Lou's argument that the lack of disagreement always signifies positioning *(4)*. Matt takes the argument up to a more general level to indicate that the rule doesn't always hold, to which Lou agrees *(5)*. However, Lou argues that given the specifics of *this* situation, the rule does hold. We can see that articulating the undrawn but relevant conclusion in this dialogue has important implications for how certain communication processes may be evaluated both immediately and in the future. Getting Lou's agreement that participation does not always require disagreement may be a premise for a future argument of Matt's about team communications.

Problem: Barriers to Effective Action Exist
Framing Opportunity: Find New Angles and Move Others to Act

Find New Angles and Move Others to Act

As discussed in Chapter One, our behavior is so closely connected to our frames that if our frames change, so too does our behavior. When barriers to taking the most effective action exist, the framing opportunity is to find a new angle and remove the barriers through reframing. This, as any student of persuasion knows, is easier said than done. As was noted in Chapter Four, at times we can hold our frames so firmly that we literally cannot see past them.

An example comes from a community planning meeting in Santa Fe, New Mexico. A small group of community leaders and activists in Santa Fe were trying to build some cross-cultural understanding and respect. Several problems surfaced, however, during the annual planning cycle. One key problem was described by the members of the planning committee as a chairwoman who was "smothering the organization." As one member put it, "We need the leader to back off. She doesn't get it that her overwhelming domination of the planning, decision making, and task assignment for the organization is driving people away. It is stifling creativity and endangering the achievements of the entire group."

This viewpoint was also shared by the leader of the planning cycle for the upcoming year. His initial frame for the solution to the problem was reminiscent of the "I win–you lose" frame common to many proposed negotiated settlements. His goal, he said, was to "get the chairwoman out of the way," "reduce her role," and "teach her that her behavior is hurting the organization she is devoted to." As happens with most win-lose frames, this led to negative and confrontive possibilities and could have prevented the team from functioning as effectively as possible. The energy expended was all negative, and, indeed, the leader of the planning cycle found himself to be planning defensively.

Before meeting with the chairwoman, however, another member found a new angle, an alternate frame reminiscent of the win-win frame in negotiation in which both parties seek to work on a mutually satisfactory solution. According to this member, "What we all want to happen is to tap the energy and talent in the group. We want to give members an opportunity to take responsibility and grow. We want to increase the power and capacity of the whole organization to expand upon its good work." With this frame, the planning process leader had access to options not available when he had been operating with a win-lose frame. Thus barriers to effective group collaboration could be removed.

The win-win frame allowed the problematic chairwoman to join in a positive task experience while saving face. It also let the meeting leader focus on values that were widely shared, avoiding punitive action to confront unproductive behavior. By finding a new angle, he enrolled more people and created a common basis for all to act. In this instance, the leader of the planning cycle was fortunate to have new angles presented. We should learn a lesson from his experience and be sure to keep our ears open for insights that others may offer.

Getting into the Habit

To prime yourself for the high-impact opportunities we've just described, envision future situations that are likely to recur. You can do this by using past conversations and meetings to anticipate future ones and thus see where linkages might be made, sleights of hand corrected, or barriers removed. Ask yourself the following questions:

- What are my repeatable contexts?
- What are the features of these repeatable contexts?
- What sources of information or misinformation will likely surface?
- How might the issues be confused?
- How should I prepare to clarify the issues?
- What questions are likely to be asked?
- What exaggerations or fallacious reasoning might someone use to make a point?
- What obstacles to action could be presented?
- How might these obstacles be resolved?
- What questionable assumptions might be made?
- What high-impact framing opportunities are likely to occur?

Trust your intuitions. You will be able to make a surprising number of reasonably accurate predictions. Initially, as you begin to notice framing opportunities presenting themselves, you will be very conscious of your priming. But each time you reflect on a framing opportunity and then each time you act on the opportunity, you further prime yourself to take advantage of future opportunities. Through continuous priming, either through reflection and/or communication, acting on a particular kind of framing opportunity becomes habitual. The force of habit, then, helps you to respond spontaneously as if you had time to prepare.

One especially powerful example of priming for opportunity comes from the world of sports. Martina Navratilova, perhaps the greatest women's tennis player of all time, was going through a slump in the late 1980s. After a match was over, Navratilova would get down on herself for missing key shots. Eventually, she turned to another tennis great, Billie Jean King, for advice. Navratilova credits King with helping her improve her "mind game" (Stains, 1994). King taught Navratilova to prime for opportunity during a match by thinking about a missed shot immediately after it was over. Navratilova would momentarily think about the opportunity she missed; then, more importantly, she would focus on the opportunity to be seized throughout the rest of the match. It was fresh in her mind because she was primed to respond if the situation presented itself again—as it was likely to do within a match. Navratilova got out of her slump and went on to achieve her historic Wimbledon victory number nine. Her victory is testament to the importance of priming.

Learning and Priming Language

Like Robin Williams in one of his rapid-fire comedy routines, we too can communicate in certain situations without slowly pondering our words before speaking. We can also learn very complex tasks involving communication without much conscious awareness of that knowledge. Communication researchers increasingly recognize that much of our knowledge of language and communication is automatically acquired. Yet do not make the mistake of thinking that automatic behavior is mindless. Much of our automatic behavior is intentional; we monitor it even as it is outside our awareness. Psychologists Reber, Allen, and Regan (1985, p. 22) argue that "every complex knowledge acquisition task is accomplished largely in the absence of conscious control. We include here the likes of socialization, acculturation, becoming a skilled diagnostician, becoming an expert in an academic field, learning a complex game like chess or go, and acquiring a natural language. Knowledge in these cases is primarily tacit; rules are not overtly specifiable."

As an example of tacit learning, let's try an exercise with the game of tic-tac-toe. Write down the rules for the game. Once you've done that, go back and review what you've written. Have you left any rules out? When the authors conducted this as an experiment, people came up with the following rules:

1. One player begins by marking an *X* and the other marking an *O*.
2. The object of the game is to get three *X*s or three *O*s in a row, column, or diagonal.
3. Players take turns marking their *X*s and their *O*s.
4. If no one achieves three *X*s or *O*s in a row, it is considered a draw or a "cat" game.

But what would happen if you were playing tic-tac-toe and the person you were playing with selected *X* on the first turn and *O* on the second turn? Or put an *X* or *O* on the line rather than in the block? Or put an *X* and *O* in the same block? You would say, "Sorry, that's against the rules." Yet, it is likely you did not articulate those rules when first asked. You recognized them only when they were broken. What is more, it is quite likely that you were never explicitly taught those rules, yet you adhere to them when you play. You learned implicitly (tacitly) and applied this second set of rules, which was residing outside of your conscious awareness. This is the reason you and most others do not articulate those rules but recognize them only when they are violated. The violation moves the rule into your conscious awareness.

The tic-tac-toe example demonstrates tacit learning. Professor Kathy Kellerman (1992, p. 294), a communication researcher, argues that "tacit or implicit learning refers to unconscious processing, an automatic and naturally occurring cognitive activity. In tacit learning, knowledge is acquired implicitly, held tacitly, and used unconsciously." Several studies demonstrating the implicit learning of language back up Kellerman's claims. For example, when asked by a foreigner, native English speakers can determine whether a particular sentence in English is correct, even if they cannot explain why and can say only that the sentence "sounds better" (Lewicki and Hill, 1987). Indeed, without any formal training, children use intricate rules of grammar in their language long before they enter school.

Even very young children who are communicative but who do not yet have language exhibit elaborate language skills. When Anika was about eighteen months old, her verbalizations were what could only be described as "gibberish"—no words and all nonsense syllables. Yet, this gibberish had the timing and rhythm of complete sentences. Moreover, she used hand and facial gestures and vocal intonation to emphasize seemingly important parts of those "sentences." To listen to Anika was to feel as though you were being told something very important, if only you could break her code. She manifested implicit learning and use of knowledge around the "telling" or delivery of a message, though the message itself remained indecipherable. Her parents had never explicitly communicated to her the rules for sentence rhythm and timing or even vocal emphasis, yet Anika had absorbed these rules from her experience.

We too can improve our language skills in our spontaneous communications by creating the conditions for more tacit learning about framing. If we direct our attention to the myriad examples of good and bad framing that occur all around, we become students of framing. To make use of these examples, however, we must know what we are looking for. The details and examples provided here concerning basic framing tools and the problems with mixed messages should help. When you are aware of framing tools and the problems with mixed messages, you can use your knowledge in two ways.

- You can trigger unconscious learning about the actual use of these forms. For example, you can examine those metaphors that may be tired and worn, inflammatory or novel, or those whose entailments create mixed messages.
- The specific language that you notice, whether yours or someone else's, can have a priming effect on your subsequent framing attempts. Noticing interesting language forms primes our unconscious mind to use them when fashioning meaning in new situations.

Don't restrict yourself to noticing framing on the job; examine it in every aspect of your life. Framing is everywhere. Be alert to framing in the editorial and sports pages of the newspaper, in politics, in great literature, and even in the church bulletin. You will find excellent examples of framing that you can use on the job. Just keep alert for them.

Finally, as you anticipate your repeatable contexts and prime yourself for high-impact framing opportunities, you can prime for language use. You can do this by reminding yourself of a favorite story to tell, jargon you want to use or avoid, a powerful metaphor, or a useful contrast. Your conscious recall of preferred language forms will leave its mark on your unconscious, helping you prime for spontaneity.

Continued use of a powerful metaphor or favorite story also primes it for future use. Have you noticed how your ability to tell a good story often improves each time you tell it? This may reflect one secret of the effectiveness of charismatic leaders. We see them and think of their verbal gifts, but what we do not see is how they have honed their messages and use of language over time with numerous audiences and speaking opportunities. Columnist William Safire (1988) made this very point about Jesse Jackson's stirring speech during the 1988 National Convention of the Democratic Party, observing that the speech was not written, but grown. It had grown through numerous previous speaking appearances, of which the vast majority of the television audience knew little. Through these appearances, Jesse Jackson had fully primed his spontaneous use of language.

A Backward Glance at This Chapter

Our framing attempts are often unconsciously but purposely formulated and executed. To become more skillful at framing under these circumstances, we must prime for spontaneity. Though the idea of controlling a spontaneous process such as framing may seem odd at first, when we take into account that control is exerted before any speech begins, it is very logical—and useful. We can exert control at the start of the overall framing process, through controlling what resides in and predominates in our memory. In working on your ability to prime for spontaneity, remember the following:

- Priming occurs when conscious recall of some information leaves an unconscious imprint that is stored away for future use and that places us in a state of mental readiness for communicating.
- Priming occurs through reflecting and/or communicating about our mental models, which we use as reference points in evaluating situations.
- Our priming can have maximum impact when we anticipate our repeatable contexts, the routine encounters that we often take for granted.
- High-impact opportunities can also be primed by using past encounters to anticipate future ones. We can set the record straight on misleading or suppressed information, make linkages if there are apparent discontinuities, find new angles if

barriers to effective action exist, and uncover assumptions and key premises in arguments.

- Learning about the language we use in framing can be both conscious and unconscious. There are specific steps we can take to facilitate both unconscious learning and the priming of desirable language.

Effective framing is vital—just as vital as credibility—for those who wish to be excellent communicators. In the final chapter of this book, we explore the connection between framing and believability and the ways you can ensure that your framing maintains and enhances your credibility.

Chapter Eight

Establishing Credibility

What You Frame, How You Frame, and How Others Frame You

Richard Milhous Nixon, one of the most analyzed political figures of the twentieth century, died on April 22, 1994. His wildly tumultuous political life can be instructive for a number of reasons, not the least of which is the question of his credibility.

In 1960, people who listened to the debate between Nixon and John F. Kennedy on the radio thought that Nixon won; those who watched the debate on television thought that JFK won. Why the difference? Kennedy had a dynamism—a charisma—about him that made Nixon look dull by comparison. Kennedy's more dynamic style was said to greatly help his credibility and to play a factor in his victory over Nixon in the election.

Eight years later, Nixon was elected president; he was reelected in a landslide in 1972. As president, Nixon had many positive accomplishments, including a historic first trip to Communist China, the signing of agreements with Moscow to limit both offensive and defensive strategic weapons, and the creation of the Environmental Protection Agency. His credibility, however, was dealt a serious blow by Watergate. The ensuing scandal over the break-in at Democratic headquarters ultimately led to the threat of impeachment, and Nixon resigned in spite of his continued denial of culpability. His credibility plunged to an all-time low. People did not believe him because he could no longer be trusted.

In the two decades after leaving office, Nixon worked very hard to repair his image. Many believe that through the ten books that

Nixon wrote, he proved to be an astute observer of the national and international political scene. Indeed, well before his death, Nixon's understanding of political issues reemerged, and thus he regained respect in the public eye.

Credibility is a fascinating and complex phenomenon. As Nixon's case demonstrates, credibility is not an intrinsic property that some communicators have and others do not; credibility is in the eye of the beholder (O'Keefe, 1990). What you find credible, others may not. For some people, Nixon never regained credibility; for others, he never lost it.

In the social sciences, there has been great debate over the components of source credibility. Though credibility is an eye-of-the-beholder phenomenon, two basic components of credibility have consistently emerged: competence and trust. *Competence* refers to how experienced, informed, skilled, or intelligent one appears to be. *Trust* refers to how honest, open-minded, fair, or unselfish one seems. Other components, such as the charisma reflected in Kennedy's 1960 debates, are regarded as more circumstantial factors.

In this chapter, we will review what is known about source credibility and link it to your framing. We will show you that how believable you are is linked to what you frame, how you frame, and how others frame you.

What You Frame: One Part of Your Believability

Part of what people use to evaluate your believability comes from the competence you display in what you frame: the subjects about which you communicate and your expertise with respect to them (what might be referred to as your value-added quality). Various aspects of what you frame can be addressed through the concepts of perspective, problem solving, vision, and personal framing.

Taking the Long Perspective

Management science professor Elliott Jaques (1990) suggests that value-added leadership comes from the ability to frame a broader company or business perspective than that of a direct report. Jaques argues that the responsibility level of any organizational role, for managers and nonmanagers alike, can be measured in terms of the target completion time of the longest task, project, or program assigned to that role. The research on time spans suggests that real managerial and hierarchical demarcations can be set at time spans of three months, one year, two years, five years, ten years, and twenty years. Value-added leadership, then, "can come only from an individual one category higher in cognitive capacity, working one category higher in problem complexity" (Jaques, 1990, p. 131).

In communication, this implies that the leader is framing a perspective that the direct report does not have, for example, how the tasks within a three-month period fit within the scheme of a yearly plan. The leader's broader perspective provides the potential to shed new light on problems of lesser scope. All other things being equal, perspective adds value and translates to believability. Jaques goes so far as to suggest that dysfunctional overlayering in bureaucracies results from individuals reporting to others who are not substantially different in how far ahead they must think and plan and thus resent the lack of value-added leadership in problem resolution.

Framing and Problem Solving

What you frame can also enhance your believability when your framing assists in problem solving. Look at the high-impact framing opportunities discussed in the previous chapter.

- If issues are unnecessarily complex, simplify them.
- If there is misleading or suppressed information, set the record straight.
- If there are apparent discontinuities, forge linkages.
- If barriers to action exist, find new angles to remove or circumvent the barriers.

These opportunities earn their high impact because they help others solve problems. If your framing facilitates a better understanding of the problem or if it increases the quality and/or efficiency of the problem-solving process, clearly you have enhanced your believability and demonstrated value-added leadership.

Vision of the Future

A third way of achieving believability with what you frame comes from having a vision. A vision often causes people to communicate about topics or issues before their time and to earn the respect of others through a unique capacity to envision a better future.

A vision seemingly before its time can sometimes be a double-edged sword. W. Edwards Deming discovered this when he first introduced his ideas about quality to U.S. companies. After the Second World War, when industry returned to the peacetime production of consumer goods, Deming's message on quality was largely ignored. American management was in the throes of Taylorism; it was in love with assembly-line production, specialization, and other principles of scientific management.

Deming found a receptive audience for his ideas in postwar Japan, especially with Japan's chief executives. He told them: "You can produce quality. You have a method for doing it. You've learned what quality is. You must carry out consumer research, look toward the future and produce goods that will have a market years from now and stay in business. You have to do it to eat. You can send quality out and get food back" (Walton, 1986, p. 13). He also told the Japanese that "the consumer is the most important part of the production line," and Walton observes that Deming "realized [this] was a new thought to Japanese management. They had hitherto sold their wares to a captive market" (Walton, 1986, p. 14).

The "new thought" spawned quality training for the Japanese worker, real changes in Japanese manufacturing processes, and eventually, an association of quality with Japanese products. To show their appreciation, in 1951 the Japanese established the prestigious Deming Prize, to recognize accomplishments in statistical theory and application.

After some thirty years and a 1979 NBC documentary, "Whatever Happened to Good Old Yankee Ingenuity?" that profiled Deming and the success of the Japanese, Deming finally found an audience in the United States. As his case illustrates, the credibility that comes from talking about themes or issues that few others are talking about may be a long time in coming.

One final point about believability and vision statements is that we do not have to be the originators of a vision to garner credibility when talking about it. We can be the improvisers, those who make novel applications of a set of existing ideas to local conditions. If we are using a vision to meet the basic needs of employees, as discussed in Chapter Three, we are helping employees to understand the vision, see its relevance, feel others' enthusiasm, understand its fit into the culture, and see next steps. Our improvisation of a vision to fit local conditions represents value-added leadership.

Impression Management with Personal Framing

Finally, we would be remiss if we did not acknowledge that an important subject of our framing is ourselves and our own actions. Known as *impression management,* the management of our image is an often subtle art that has the potential to enhance our believability. Impression management occurs most explicitly in public communication contexts: when we introduce speakers by reviewing their credentials and accomplishments, for example, or speakers associate themselves with influential sources. As we saw in Chapter Two, however, if we hold specific identity goals, impression management also occurs in our everyday communications. If we let others know of our role in a particular project, our new ideas, our caring and concern, our priorities, our justification for some unpopular action, or our value-added activity in whatever form it may take, we are framing ourselves to gain believability.

Is there anything wrong with this? Absolutely not, which is why those who are reticent in taking credit for good work will often be urged to promote themselves more. However, self-promotion can get out of hand; we have all heard comments such as "Jim's in love with himself," or, "May's biggest fan is May." Negative attributions from too much self-promotion occur when perceptions about our contributions are not shared. The old adage holds—give credit where credit is due.

To summarize, credibility that comes from what we frame can come from many sources: the perspective we supply, high-impact framing opportunities that help in problem solving, our vision, things that we are framing that others are not, and appropriately framing ourselves.

How You Frame and Gain Believability

Believability regarding what you frame tends to center on issues of competence and what added value you bring; believability regarding how you frame tends to center on matters of trust and conviction. Here we discuss two key factors in communicating a vision with authority: speaking style and believability framing.

The Importance of Speaking Style

Let's begin with a test. How do you react to the following two sentences?

Sentence A:

"Well, I think we can, uh, and will be kind of competitive in those new markets; definitely we could do that?"

Sentence B:

"We can and will be competitive in those new markets."

Both sentences A and B frame a projected response to new markets as competitive; thus, strictly speaking, the framing is the same. Yet sentence A is a tentative, uncertain statement, because it contains what are known as "powerless" speech forms. Linguistic anthropologist William O'Barr and his colleagues, Bonnic Erickson, E. Allan Lind, and Bruce Johnson (Erickson, Lind, Johnson, and O'Barr, 1978, p. 271) have identified several of these forms:

- *Hedges:* language that reduces the force of an assertion by allowing for exceptions or by avoiding commitments, such as "sort of," "a little," and "kind of"
- *Intensifiers:* language that increases or emphasizes the force of an assertion, such as "very," "definitely," "very definitely," and "surely"
- *Hesitations:* "meaningless" expressions, such as "oh, well," "let's see," "so, you see," "uh," "um," and "you know"
- *Questioning forms:* use of rising question intonation at the end of what would otherwise normally be declarative sentences, such as "I weigh 125?" or "Definitely we could do that?"

In a program of research that investigated the use of powerless speech forms in actual dialogue in court settings, O'Barr and his colleagues identified a "powerless style" as comprising the language forms just listed (and as seen in Sentence A) and a "powerful" style characterized by a less frequent use of these features (as in Sentence B). In one study, males and females heard the testimony of either a male or female witness who used either the powerful or powerless style to deliver the same substantive evidence. Regardless of whether the testimony was presented in transcript or through audiotape, and regardless of whether the witness or the rating audience was male or female, the powerful style resulted in greater perceived credibility of the witness (Erickson, Lind, Johnson, and O'Barr, 1978).

For more evidence of the importance of speaking style, one has only to look at the double murder trial of O. J. Simpson and to compare the testimony of the police detectives with that of Brian "Kato" Kaelin, the Simpson houseguest who was with him on the night of the murders. Kaelin is not an experienced witness, and his testimony was rife with hesitations, hedges, intensifiers, and questioning intonations. The police officers, on the other hand, are veterans of numerous trials. They have been trained in answering questions with a powerful speaking style and minimizing potentially damaging testimony simply by limiting verbiage around the admission of mistakes or contradictions. The strength of their testimony versus that of Kato's underscores the importance of speaking style.

It is safe to assume that many of those in the Simpson trial cultivated the powerful speech that they used; it did not come to them naturally. The consistency with which the police officers, for example, exhibited powerful speaking styles is testament to the learned nature of this manner of speaking. So if you are a chronic user of powerless speech forms, be reassured that it is possible to eliminate them from your language and speaking style. If they dominate your speaking style, it may take some effort to eliminate them completely. But through awareness and priming of how you want to frame a subject, it is possible to change.

As research and common sense tell us, to the extent we can eliminate powerless speech forms from our speaking style, we will increase our believability. Consistent use of hedges, intensifiers, hesitations, and questioning forms tends to show a lack of self-confidence, powerlessness, or a lack of conviction, all of which detract from our credibility. Certainly, there are times when we harbor doubts about the meanings we manage, such as when we have scant information on a subject. This should, however, be the exception and not the rule. If we don't have the conviction of our beliefs, how can we expect others to?

For many, it is impossible to divorce what someone says from how they say it, whether in a trial, on the job, or in any emotional venue. This connection is critical: what gets said matters little if the speaker is not believed. Believability is often decided on a subliminal, unconscious level. Often, people can't say why they believe someone, just that they do. "Powerless" versus "powerful" speaking styles are one factor in their unconscious decisions.

Believability Framing

The second argument related to believability and how we frame is that we can improve our believability by effectively framing our frames. In the following conversation, Teri and her junior manager, Page, are discussing a division manager who has complained about their plant's poor representation at an upcoming TQM statistics training session. Page, who is the plant's TQM manager, doesn't feel that the course is a good fit. She also does not want to take the issue up directly with the division manager because to do so would violate a confidence. (She was told of the division manager's comments by one of the two people to whom he made the remarks.) Page wants the plant manager to write a note to another more sympathetic member of the organization's hierarchy to explain why the plant will not attend. Teri feels that Page should either send someone to the course or confront the division leader directly.

Page: I'll tell you the facts. Do you want to know what I really think it is? I think they already signed the contract. It's a lot of money. I think that nobody wants to go back and either try to get out of the contract or modify it better to meet our needs or question whether or not the need is there.

Teri: I know. But looking at it objectively, it will just hurt Atlanta for a long time.

Page: I would like to deal with it in this way. Say this is what our position is and this is why we don't think this is right. To me, what's going on here is really against Total Quality, okay? He is trying to instill fear in folks to force them to do something. And that's just not right.

[*Silence.*]

Teri: You have got to look at which is going to be better for the long run. It's going to be hard to get that negative perception off of us because the first thing will always be, "No one went to the training, so how can you possibly be any good? You're not getting that information. Somehow you missed out along the way." Atlanta will always be the one that's got a question. We'll never be up in the headlines of how well we're doing with Total Quality, no matter how well we do, no matter how right you are, and all those things. And I know this division manager. I know how he operates. He's very much in the old style of it. Traditional. So, he'll play the game. He'll play the politics. He'll put the pressure on. He'll plug the fear in. He'll make the comments. He is very much with the comments and the jabs. And that will forever be out in the system, and we don't need that. So we have to go and solve it (with the division manager), or we have to send someone to the training session.

Teri and Page do their best to frame the issues in specific ways: both use metaphors, contrast, and spin. Teri appears especially adept in her use of language. Consider her metaphors for the division manager and her dramatic use of "parallel form" in the similar sounding sentences she constructs to present them: "So, he'll play the game. He'll play the politics. He'll put the pressure on. He'll plug the fear in. He'll make the comments. He is very much with the comments and the jabs."

She uses negative spin when she says, "It's gonna be hard to get that negative perception off of us." She continues her use of spin and combines it with contrast and metaphor in stating, "Atlanta will always be the one that's got a question. We'll never be up in the headlines of how well we're doing with Total Quality."

But there is more framing going on here than meets the eye. In problem-solving and decision-making situations especially, arguments and cases are constructed based upon premises or key propositions. If the premises of an argument reflect an appealing frame or interpretation, then acceptance of the framed premise quite logically leads to some decisions and actions over others. For example, if you accept the premise that smoking causes cancer, then you tend to support decisions that ban smoking in offices, airplanes, and restaurants. If you do not accept that premise, or you believe another premise, such as smokers have rights too, then you tend not to support decisions that ban smoking.

Taking away all of the extraneous conversation, you can see at least one framed premise in each of Teri's and Page's speaking turns. What is less visible in the dialogue is the manner in which Page and Teri then frame their already framed premises as factual, objective, not legitimate, or real.

Speaker	Dialogue	Premise/Frame of the Frame	Explanation
Page	*I think they already signed the contract. (implying a financial motive to force attendance).*	Premise	Framing fact
	I'll tell you the facts.	Frame of the frame	
Teri	*It will just hurt Atlanta for a long time.*	Premise	Framing objectivity
	But looking at it objectively.	Frame of the frame	
Page	*He [the division manager] is trying to instill fear in folks. What's going on here is really against Total Quality, okay?*	Premise	Framing the lack of legitimacy
		Frame of the frame	

Speaker	Dialogue	Premise/Frame of the Frame	Explanation
Teri	*It's going to be hard to get that negative perception off of us because the first thing will always be, "No one went to the training, so how can you possibly be any good?"*	Frame of the frame	Framing what is real

Page and Teri engage in a kind of frame of their frames as they jockey to position their premise as the basis of the decision. Like a close horse race in which the bobbing of the horses' heads shows the lead changing back and forth, each framed premise is positioned relative to the others to try to put it in the lead. The speakers are trying to achieve believability from one of three sources, which they then mold into a frame: truthfulness or reality, objectivity, or legitimacy. The next sections discuss these frames and how you can use them to increase your believability.

Truth and Reality Framing

> *Function:* To Establish a Claim to Truth
> *Use It Because:* You Believe in the Truthfulness of a Particular Claim
> *Avoid It When:* You Know the Claim to Be False

Truth and reality framing, often simply called reality framing, occurs when speakers explicitly claim that their framing of events is "the way things are" (Deetz, 1985). One could argue that truth and reality framing occurs any time a declarative statement is made. However, some reality framing is much more explicit, such as when we link our frames to what is "real" or when we emphatically assert that the frame represents "what is." For example, Page's first premise in the excerpt ("I think they already signed the contract") has a reality frame attached to it when Page prefaces it with, "I'll tell you the facts. Do you want to know what I really think it is?" If your framed premise leads others to perceive you as having a firmer grasp of reality or more direct access to the truth, then quite naturally it is seen as a more credible piece of information upon which to base a decision.

We are most often driven to use truth and reality frames when we believe strongly in the frames and arguments that we are advancing. Thus, while all of our frames are suitable for reality framing, usually key frames or central ideas receive this type of additional framing. Framing something as a fact or the truth is one way to call attention to the key frames in our arguments and the key frames upon which to base decisions.

Have you ever observed people who just seem to have a confident air about them, sound very convincing, and speak authoritatively? Listen carefully to radio talk show hosts who have developed reputations for persuasiveness or who have large followings with a particular social or political point of view. Listen to the television evangelists known for the power of their inspirational preaching. These people are experts in truth and reality framing. They do four things effectively:

1. They use conjugations of the verb *to be,* using *is, are,* and *be* in key statements such as "He is confident in his abilities" and "We are lost without her vision."
2. Much as we have seen in the examples, they frame their pronouncements in terms of facts, truth, or reality. Phrases such as, "The simple truth is . . . ," "The facts are . . . ," and "The reality is . . ." are typical.
3. They avoid powerless speech forms, especially hedges, hesitations, and questioning intonations.
4. They sound authoritative by using nonverbal emphasis and stress in key places for dramatic effect: for example, "I *know* the reason for this letter"; "His departure is a *tremendous* loss to this company."

Verbally and nonverbally, then, they reinforce the verbal "this is truth" frame.

For a business example of reality framing, consider the following. Brent, a department manager, is talking with Meryl, one of his female team managers. Brent is coaching Meryl about her communication style. Note the forms of reality framing (in italics):

(1) *Brent:* A lot of times, when you're talking about losses or problems that they're having on lines, you speak in almost an apologetic fashion. I think you need to get to the point where you're really comfortable with what they are talking about.

(2) *Meryl:* Okay.

(3) *Brent:* And I think the reason—or *I know the reason*— why I want you to do that is because there is prejudice out there about women not understanding technical stuff.

(4) *Meryl:* Well, *that's a fact.* A lot of times I don't explain it, not because I can't, but because it takes a lot of time. *It's obvious* I need to do that from a credibility viewpoint, though, if for no other reason.

(5) *Brent:* *Absolutely.*

There is a kind of spiraling of truth and reality framing in this excerpt. Brent appears tentative when he initially offers reasons for Meryl's communication style ("I think the reason . . .") However, he amends that quickly and verbally stresses "I know the reason . . . ," framing his thinking on that point as the truth *(3)*. Meryl responds with her confirmation of the stereotype of women with a frame of fact ("Well, that's a fact" *[4]*). She also frames the need to change as obvious, again making a factual claim. Finally, Brent confirms Meryl's pronouncement of fact about the obvious need to change with his own pronouncement of "absolutely."

A rather obvious cautionary note about truth and reality framing is that saying something doesn't necessarily make it so. Truth and reality framing is claim, not fact. There can be multiple realities or versions of the truth depending upon who is doing the perceiving.

Certainly, differences in information or experience can contribute to the different perspectives that we bring to our framing. Conscious or unconscious, the presence of bias and self-interest also alters our perception of events. Indeed, it is well recognized that biases predispose us to see situations in ways that others with different biases and interests would not. At times, we may be motivated by self-interest that masquerades as a concern for the truth. The discovery by others of our self-interested framing immediately detracts from our believability. Moreover, it becomes a part of the context that others use in interpreting our future communications.

Objectivity Framing

Function:	To Establish Your Fairness or Objectivity
Use It Because:	You Believe You Have Been as Impartial as You Can Be
Avoid It When:	You Know You Are Biased, and You Are Claiming Objectivity for the Sake of Appearances

In addition to truth and reality framing, often speakers will make additional claims about themselves or their positions so as to appear to be neutral or unbiased (Deetz, 1985). The objectivity frame is a claim in which one asserts one's fairness, neutrality, independence in judgment, or freedom from bias due to personal or other interests.

Consider the following example. Two managers, Raleigh and Dexter, are talking about another employee, named John, who committed an infraction by failing to report a chemical spill. Examine Raleigh's and Dexter's objectivity framing, which we have put in italics.

Raleigh: John was very apologetic and knew that he had done wrong. He said he forgot that he took care of the problem and went down to the fire inspector to make sure the pH was right but didn't make any records of it. He didn't let anybody know about it, and I told him that I had to know. A report had to be made. I told him that as far as I was concerned, one more slip-up and then you would take some severe action with him.

Dexter: I don't know if I can wait one more. I have bent over backwards *to be fair* to this guy. But the potential for disaster there is so great that if there is any single place in the plant where disaster can strike, it's right there. We have got a problem.

Raleigh: I know what you're saying. It's a very sensitive area and *in all fairness* to him, he's got to get help. You know he had a weird look in his eyes leaving Friday afternoon. I couldn't swear that I could smell it, but I knew that his breath wasn't right. It was either medication or something that shouldn't have been there. He wasn't sick, as far as I know.

Dexter: Let's you and Scott and I talk at the end of the day.

Dexter and Raleigh accompany their arguments with objectivity framing to make themselves and their positions appear neutral. Objectivity framing, which is clearly valued in our society, makes it appear as though the individual is acting with the best interests of everyone in mind. No doubt you encounter it with some frequency. How many times, for example, have you heard, "in all fairness," "objectively speaking," or "putting aside all self-interest"?

Objectivity framing can also be accomplished with "hard numbers," statistical manipulations, or in general, quantitative data of any kind (Deetz, 1985). The appearance of numbers, combined with such conventional wisdom as "the numbers don't lie" or "the numbers tell the story," gives the appearance of objectivity. Yet, in commenting on objectivity framing through numerical data, Mark Twain once said, "There are three kinds of lies: lies, damned lies, and statistics!" Certainly, we are not dismissing quantitative data as necessarily biased. However, we would put most quantitative data in the category of claims about reality, which also make such data suitable for objectivity framing. In the following example, Carolyn questions the statistical claims that her staff member, Gerald, is making:

Gerald: We can show a 15 percent increase in production from last year at this time. That's got to say something about the new technology.

Carolyn: Yeah, but our systems were shut down for some eight weeks last year between breakdowns and the technology transfer. Plus, we have had very little down time this year. Somehow you have got to recalculate gains based on percent operating time and percent downtime.

The ease with which Carolyn takes apart Gerald's claim of 15 percent increase in production demonstrates that while quantitative data may indeed appear objective, it is but one claim to reality.

The same cautions about when to avoid truth and reality framing also apply to objectivity framing. We may be motivated by self-interest that masquerades as a concern for neutrality or objectivity. One thing is sure: a leader who is not perceived as acting in a manner relatively free of self or organizational interests gains little from objectivity framing.

Such was the case with Stuart, a very controlling and opinionated manager. Stuart was under great pressure to change his management style to become more participative. He thought that participation meant not telling his people directly what to do. Indirectly, he would indicate what should be done through framing himself as objective and then raising an alternative way—his way— to think about the issue. If people did not immediately see the merits of his alternative way of thinking, he would pursue it until they did. His team of managers grew increasingly frustrated, as reflected in the following conversation. June and Stuart are discussing what technicians need to know about the unit costs of shipments out of the plant:

> *June:* Sure, I think they need to know a lot more than unit cost.
> But unit cost is meaningless to them if they don't know
> what they can do about it.
> *Stuart:* Yeah, of course there's the risk on the other side of knowing way too much. *I'm trying to follow all kinds of things.*
> *June:* Well, I don't think they need to follow a bunch of things.
> I just think they need to be aware of some things like
> when you spend $3,000 detention a month, what kind of
> impact that's going to have on unit cost.

Stuart introduces an objectivity frame when he says, "I'm trying to follow all kinds of things." With that statement, he appears to play devil's advocate. When playing devil's advocate, you can make a counterargument without necessarily owning it, which is what Stuart does. He refrains from directly owning the statement, "there's the risk, on the other side, of knowing way too much," implying a more neutral stance. Notice, however, how June rejects Stuart's neutrality frame outright when she says rather directly, "Well, I don't think they need to follow a bunch things." June tells us that she recognizes this to be another one of Stuart's games and that Stuart is really against communicating knowledge of unit costs even though he never directly says so.

In keeping with June's experience, a consultant to the plant told the authors of this book, "People don't seem to trust Stuart because he frequently has his mind made up before discussing an issue. Yet, he tries to show that he is open when he isn't." Stuart has a credibility problem, due in part to a discrepancy between what he says and what he does. As noted in Chapter Six, people tend to believe the message that the speaker is perceived to have less control over or that is more consistent with past behavior. In this case, Stuart's playing devil's advocate is seen as a manipulative game and consistent with a controlling management style that has been attributed to him in the past.

Legitimacy Framing

Function:	To Render Legitimate Through Appeals to Principle, Authority, Practice, or Evidence
Use It Because:	Additional Justification Is Needed to Rationalize a Course of Action.
Avoid It When:	Sources Are Falsely Legitimate or Less Legitimate than Others.

A third believability framing tool attaches importance to frames through appeals to principle (values), practices, authority, or evidence (Deetz, 1985). We call these *legitimacy frames* because the speaker rationalizes a course of action by invoking another credible source. For example, one could justify a frame by appealing to an organizational vision or mission, societal, organizational, or personal standards and practices, or a conventionally accepted body of evidence. By invoking an accepted standard, the speaker gains a yardstick with which to measure a subject's consistency, appropriateness, effectiveness, or other form of legitimacy.

In the following example, Peter is a new manager who has been assigned to Kent's module. Kent is describing his management style for Peter and justifies it on the basis of his personal values:

Kent: One of the things *I place real high value* in is not managing by default, saying I believe something when I don't or do something when I don't believe it's right. If I lost an argument with my boss, I will not defer to him. *It's not me,* and I won't default under any circumstance. If we get to working an issue, I would expect the same of my employees—to carry it out the same way and not defer to me. That's the way I run my business. It might not be right, but *that's the way I've been programmed. It's my personal code.*

Peter: I hear what you're saying.

Kent uses several legitimacy frames with expressions such as "I place real high value," "It's not me," "the way I've been programmed," and "It's my personal code," all to justify the frame of his management style as "not managing by default." Thus, his legitimacy frames are based on his own claims about personal values and sense of self.

Legitimacy framing should be used cautiously when there may be competing sets of standards or principles upon which to base legitimacy. Some of these standards may be more legitimate than others, and multiple claims to legitimacy have to be negotiated. Thus, one must ask, whose standards and principles are to be applied in legitimacy framing?

Consider the following example. Elaine is a team leader who questions one of her technicians, Burt, about a goal he has set. Burt uses intuition as his source of legitimacy:

(1) *Elaine:* Why wouldn't you be as aggressive for this goal as you have been for the others? Do you think something's going to happen to the furnace here?

(2) *Burt:* No, I didn't think in terms of the furnace, quite frankly. It's just a *gut feel* to improve around the same percentage as we had on the other two areas here.

(3) *Elaine:* We have to talk about this some. Do you still think it is right? Or should we be more aggressive and set it higher?

(4) *Burt:* I think it would be right to be more aggressive in terms of the way that we're setting our other goals in other areas.

Burt justifies the goal he set based upon a "gut feel" legitimacy frame, which Elaine appears to reject with her somewhat indirect statement, "We have to talk about this some," followed by a not-so-subtle leading question, "Do you still think it is right? Or should we be more aggressive and set it higher?" *(3)*. It's not clear from this exchange whether Elaine just rejects the "gut feel" frame out of hand or simply feels that it is not warranted in this case.

Reliance on intuition has had a rather checkered past in the history of management, as it was often framed as "too soft" or "feminine" in comparison to rational thinking. Note, however, that the manager who rejects the reliance on the intuition in this case is female. The stereotype does not hold; this fact reinforces for us that we must analyze each frame as it is used.

Communicating Your Vision with Authority

In Chapter Three, we suggested that leaders should develop communication goals to address several needs that employees have with regard to an organizational vision:

- Understand the vision
- See the vision's relevance to one's job or role
- Feel others' enthusiasm for the vision
- See the vision's fit to the existing culture
- See next steps in implementing the vision

Communication goals addressing these needs will be ineffective without the use of believability frames (summarized in Table 8.1). Believability frames are critical because the heart of communicating a vision is to say that the current state of affairs must be changed. Thus, you must be able to define what is real and what is not real with respect to existing circumstances. You must be able to legitimize the vision with the need for change. You must be seen as acting objectively with everyone's best interest at heart. And, in truth, you must own the vision.

The authority with which you communicate a vision is ultimately a moral one. It is to be hoped that your moral compass will direct you to use reality frames when you believe strongly in a frame and to avoid them when you know a frame to be false or misleading. Your moral compass should direct you to use objectivity frames when you believe you have been as impartial as you can be and to avoid them when there is bias and too much self-interest. It should alert you to times in which you might be managing for the sake of appearance. Finally, your moral compass should direct you to use legitimacy frames when additional justification is needed to rationalize a course of action but avoid them when the justifications are falsely legitimate.

The consequence of a failure of your moral compass is lost credibility, either in the impression of your competence or of your trustworthiness. When your credibility is lost, so is your ability to

Table 8.1. Believability Frames.

Type of Frame	Truth and Reality	Objectivity	Legitimacy
Function	To establish a claim to truth or what is real.	To establish your fairness or objectivity.	To render legitimate through appeals to principle, authority, practice, or evidence.
Use it because	You believe in the truthfulness of a particular claim.	You believe you have been as impartial as can be.	Additional justification is needed to rationalize a course of action.
Avoid it when	You know the claim to be false.	You know you are biased, and you are claiming objectivity for the sake of appearance.	Sources are falsely legitimate or less legitimate than others.

foster the vision, as the following conversation demonstrates. Rich, a manager with aspirations to be a plant manager, has been aggressive in advancing the philosophies of team-based systems and the need for diversity. Yet, the feedback he receives from Luke, one of his key managers, suggests that both Rich's credibility and his aspirations are in some trouble.

(1) *Luke:* The women managers here in this module are saying, "I hear what he says he wants to do, but I'm not really sure I believe it because of what I'm hearing."

(2) *Rich:* Well, some of those old stories—so that you know what is going on—they are not stories. They are true. I had five secretaries reporting to me in Industrial Engineering. And they were all women who were not doing their jobs. I went in working that real hard, and they didn't like that at all. And so they reacted with, "I can't work with that guy."

(3) *Luke:* It's more than that, though. Some stories are floating around about you being in the company of other managers—at least this is what got back to me—and you made some remarks that could be interpreted as being negative towards women in general. They got to the women second hand.

(4) *Rich:* [*Laughs.*]

(5) *Luke:* And there's been some things going around the circle of team managers suggesting that you're not as supportive as you seem to be on the surface.

(6) *Rich:* Well, I can understand if the women had this framework of "I can't work with women" and that they heard some comments that could be construed negatively. Well, I think the thing that I need to do is spend more time with them, particularly with Penny, Alice, and Karen so that they get more comfortable. And we get more comfortable with each other.

(7) *Luke:* There's lots of this that has come to me third hand. And it's really hard to tell how much it has changed in the translation.

(8) *Rich:* Yeah, okay, let's move on.

This is a curious conversation. Luke delivers to Rich evidence of some rather serious charges being made. Even if untrue, the rumor potential could be quite damaging. Yet, Rich laughs off the suggestion that he made disparaging remarks against women, and his remedy is to just generally spend more time with them *(6)*. Finally, after Luke inserts a disclaimer about third-hand information *(7)*, Rich changes the subject *(8)*. Rich does not seem to grasp the fact that all of his believability frames about diversity and valuing women especially are being questioned in Luke's feedback to him. If Rich does grasp the import of this feedback, he certainly does not let on. Has Rich made disparaging remarks about women in the past, as the stories suggest? If he hasn't, does he treat seriously the idea that others, particularly women, are now questioning his credibility? Where is Rich's moral compass? What does he value?

A more prudent response would begin with finding out more information from Luke about the nature of the stories, the things the team managers are saying specifically about Rick's lack of supportiveness and the specific reactions of the women. It would also be wise to find out whether this is tied to any other work issues. Also, since Luke is a key subordinate, Rich might discuss with him ideas about how to manage the meaning of these rumors directly with the women. The opportunity to manage meaning is knocking loudly on Rich's door. Unless Rich manages the meaning of these rumors, he is letting others frame his management style. Worse yet, his future framing on diversity issues will be questioned.

All three believability framing tools are pervasive in communication in which there is discussion and debate. Though we use them strategically to assert our view of reality over another, we often use them spontaneously and unconsciously. We can become more conscious of our believability frames simply by paying attention to those key phrases that signal their use, such as "in fact," "in truth," "in all fairness," "speaking objectively," "it's not right because of this standard or that principle." You can do this as you prepare remarks for an anticipated meeting by asking yourself these questions:

- Is what I intend to say factual?
- Is it truthful?
- Am I objective in saying it?
- Is it legitimate? On what grounds?

By simply moving the questions into the past tense, you can also use them to review an encounter you have just had or even a long previous encounter. Ask yourself:

- Was what I said factual?
- Was what I said truthful?
- Was I objective in what I said?
- Was what I said legitimate? On what grounds was it legitimate?

This level of reflection is useful because the questions remind us that we are making claims about truth, reality, objectivity, or legitimacy in an attempt to be persuasive and argue effectively for our visions or other communication goals.

In addition, a deeper level of self-analysis is useful. Continuous reflection on who you are and what you're about provides the best conditions for evaluating whether your framing for others is truthful, real, objective, and legitimate. We agree with management writers James Kouzes and Barry Posner, who state in their book *Credibility* (1993) that one of the first steps to gaining credibility, especially as regards an organizational vision, is to know your self. The odyssey to knowing your self is not a momentary reflection about one conversation or another. Instead, it is a continuous and renewable commitment you make to yourself to

- *Develop your own value base.* Ask yourself, "What do I stand for?" "What really matters to me?"
- *Understand your personal and organizational purpose.* Ask yourself, "Why am I here?" "What is my purpose in life?" "What is my purpose in this role in this organization?"
- *Look to the future to see what opportunities might be realized.* Ask yourself the miracle question: "If my organization were operating effectively, what would it look like?"
- *Examine the past and the stories it contains about your effectiveness, your character, and your mental models.* Ask yourself, "What do I do well?" "What do I do not so well?" "How does my character shape my response to situations?" and "What are my prevailing mental models?" "What assumptions am I making, and are they valid?"

If, through your efforts, you are clear about yourself and your beliefs, your clarity will be reflected in your believability framing. As we saw in Chapter Two, in discussing underdeveloped mental models, trouble awaits you if you lack clarity. This point is elaborated further in the next section.

How Others Frame You—and Your Believability

What and how you frame are extremely important to your credibility. So, too, is how others frame you. No matter how sincere you believe your efforts to be, they are not enough if others hold negative frames of you.

To reinforce the importance of others' frames, we can look to the example of Stephen Wolf, the outgoing CEO of UAL Corporation, parent of United Airlines. When Wolf came on board, United had the oldest fleet of the major carriers and no clear strategy. During his seven-year reign, Wolf and his team put into place a fleet plan, a route structure, and a service strategy. The fact that labor costs were not in line led to an unpopular stance toward labor. Thus, when United was purchased by various employee groups, they demanded that Wolf and two of his top managers resign. Union leaders nominated former Chrysler vice chairman Gerald Greenwald, who had no experience running airlines. Greenwald was chosen in part because, as one machinist said of him, "everybody says he's a good people person" (Labich, 1994).

What contributes to others' frames of us? Perhaps the first thing to keep in mind is that when others frame us, they rarely do so on the basis of a single event. Others frame us based upon our patterns of behavior over time, drawing conclusions about who we are and what we stand for, whether our words and actions are consistent with one another, and how much of what we bring to the table matches their interests.

It is fitting that we return to Lee Iacocca to demonstrate the importance of a pattern. Early in this book, we hailed Iacocca's performance before Congress and quoted from Iacocca's best-selling autobiography. Iacocca's sparkling image might have remained intact had he continued his retirement. But in 1995, along with billionaire Kirk Kerkorian, Iacocca was part of a hostile takeover bid for Chrysler. This brought Iacocca back into the spotlight where few questioned his skill as a pitchman and advocate, but many questioned his credibility when his entire career was considered. For example, an article in *Newsweek* (Levin, 1995) described two Iacoccas. There was the public Iacocca, known from his impressive leadership during the Chrysler bailout, his Statue of Liberty campaign, and his popular autobiography. But there was also the Iacocca that only a few industry insiders knew—a money-hungry man with an enormous ego, quick to take credit for others' good work. Given this dichotomy, it is not surprising that Detroit's coolness toward Iacocca's return was widely reported.

Why such negative sentiment? There were charges of a distorted account of his departure from Ford (an account crucial to his myth of revenge against a boss who wronged him), the lobbying of Richard Nixon to block mandatory air bags, preoccupation with his celebrity, concern for slick advertising over quality, jealousy of Chrysler's other rising stars, and his stance as a most reluctant backer of Chrysler's reorganization into teams (Levin, 1995). In this example, we can see how the perspective of time shows our past decisions to be wise or foolish, reveals the inconsistencies between what we say and do, and gives others a truer picture of what we bring to the table despite our claims to the contrary.

The second thing to keep in mind is that reality is socially constructed, as we saw in Chapter One. While everyone forms individual impressions, who you are and what you stand for will likely be the subject of discussion and debate. Your image, then, is co-constructed in the numerous conversations others have about you. This occurs most often when others have a need to make sense of your present behavior because it conflicts with attributions that have been made in the past.

Two management professors, Chao Chen and James Meindl (1991), conducted a fascinating case study of Donald Burr of People Express that showed that people strive for consistency in their judgments of leaders over time yet not at the expense of accounting for the ups and downs of performance. Burr founded People Express Airline in 1981 and experienced successive periods of great success, mixed performance, and failure leading to an eventual merger with Texas Air. Through an analysis of media clips, Chen and Meindl were able to demonstrate that early media portraits of Burr as a preacher with messianic zeal gave way to fanaticism and rigidity in later accounts. Such a reconstruction permits others to retain a certain consistency in their perceptions, showing how the image of a preacher has both an upside and a downside without having to sacrifice the early image of preacher altogether.

The lessons about credibility here suggest that others will be driven to explain rather than overlook key events affecting us, such as weak performance for which we are responsible. However, there will be a preference for consistency between past and present attributions. Credibility, again, is in the eye of the beholder.

A Backward Glance at This Chapter

This chapter addressed how we gain believability through our framing. Three factors influence believability: what you frame, how you frame, and how others frame you. We should bear in mind the following points about these three factors:

- Believability in framing can come from the perspective you supply, from high-impact framing opportunities that help in problem solving, from your vision (what you are framing that others are not), and from framing yourself and your own actions.
- Believability that comes from how you frame is influenced first by your speaking style. Major factors in speaking style include the presence (or absence) of powerless speech forms such as hedges, hesitations, intensifiers, and question intonations.
- How you frame is also influenced by three types of believability framing that build upon each other. *Truth and reality frames* focus on establishing what is real, truthful, or what exists. *Objectivity frames* are concerned with establishing our neutrality, objectivity, or the ability to balance multiple interests. *Legitimacy frames* are concerned with justifying our frames from standards, principles, practices, or a body of evidence.
- Believability frames are powerful tools and need to be used carefully. They are especially important for those leaders espousing a vision.
- Leaders must have a strong moral compass in place to guide them in their use of believability frames; without that, their credibility will suffer.
- Believability that comes from how others frame you suggests that perceptions count and that perceptions over time count even more. Others will frame you in their conversations because they will be driven to make sense of your current behavior in light of the past. In doing so, people are inclined to want to be consistent in their attributions.

As we can see, the art of framing is both critical and complex. Fortunately, we can break it down into concrete skills that can be learned and polished over time. The Epilogue presents some final thoughts about the importance and possibilities of framing.

Epilogue: Framing in Action

The September 11, 1994, headline of the *Cincinnati Enquirer* (Wolff, 1994) said it all: "Going, Going . . . Still There!" The Department of Energy (DOE) and the Fernald Environmental Restoration Management Corporation (FERMCO), the people who produced the three-legged stool vision metaphor we discussed in Chapter Five, had planned an elaborate public ceremony around the implosion of Fernald's tallest structure, a seven-story building. From 1953 to 1989, the Fernald plant processed uranium metal used for nuclear weapons, and Building 7 housed "green salt," deadly chemicals used in uranium processing. The public demolition of the building was to have been a symbolic turning point in Fernald's cleanup efforts. The meanings management hoped to manage with this event were three: the clean-up was being performed ahead of schedule, under budget, and safely. In changing Fernald's skyline, they would take a step in changing a contentious history with stakeholders, a history marked by class-action lawsuits in which Fernald workers and nearby residents had been awarded millions of dollars in compensation for medical and emotional problems associated with the contaminated site.

Government officials, Department of Energy officials, Fernald employees, nearby residents, and members of the aggressive citizens watchdog groups monitoring Fernald's clean up all gathered for the celebration. Before the implosion, an assistant secretary of energy hailed this event as "one of the most dramatic depictions of how the entire world had changed in the wake of the Cold War." The DOE plant manager said he hoped that Fernald would "set a good example nationally" (Feiertag, 1994).

Then the moment all had waited for finally came. A series of loud pop-pop-pop's sounded as fifty explosive devices went off in close succession. A cloud of mist and smoke swirled from the ground only to reveal that the 120-foot structure had dropped 45 feet—and then tilted at a fifteen-degree angle to the northwest. "Going, going . . . still there" indeed!

The crowd was silenced. DOE and Fernald officials on the podium were stunned and embarrassed. The assistant secretary of energy had joked in his early remarks that he had two speeches prepared, one in case the demolition worked and one in case it didn't. But he hurriedly left the stage after the failed demolition and canceled his press conference. The Maryland construction firm on board to conduct the implosion had never had one fail before. This was small consolation. Fernald's public affairs program had prepared senior managers well for the expected takedown; they never even envisioned its failure. The best that any of the officials at the podium could come up with was a remark from a DOE official who said, "This is a credit to the construction workers of the forties" (Wolff, 1994).

If the officials at the podium were at a loss to supply meaning to this event, Fernald's watchdog groups were not. Right after the failed implosion, the head of Fernald Residents for Environmental Safety and Health (FRESH) said, "We really had our hopes up for this. It would have been a 'visual aid' for us, saying, 'Yes, we're on our way'" (Wolff, 1994). The day after the event, another member of FRESH said, "I think the biggest accident they'll ever have out here is to do something right the first time." The president of another local citizens' group for environmental action said that the failed implosion was a metaphor for all of Fernald: "We've constantly been assured by government agencies and operators of plants like this that everything is safe. The failure even to knock a building down tells us that human technology is fallible and can represent danger to the public" (Bricking, 1994). It was clear that Fernald's watchdog groups were ready to manage the meaning for the implosion, even when Fernald officials were not.

Building 7 would not be brought down until several days later. Were it not for management's response to the whole event, this would be a story about missed opportunities. After all, September 11, 1994, was nothing short of a public relations disaster. But public affairs staff, led by their director, asked of themselves immediately afterward, "What are the lessons learned?" And they realized very quickly that regardless of when Building 7 came down, the meanings they had hoped to manage on that fateful September day still applied. The clean-up was ahead of schedule. The clean-up was under budget. And the clean-up was proceeding safely. Management accepted the advice of public affairs, which was to proactively manage this message. The members of management did this, however, not for "damage control" but to communicate a message in which they strongly believed. They would also show a commitment to continuing the dialogue with stakeholders in good times and in bad. Analysis of subsequent media accounts not only revealed that Fernald's message had gotten through but also that the complexity of the takedown engendered some compassion from the news media. What did not make the news reports was that the travails of Building 7 also became a rallying point for employees.

The lessons of Building 7 are a fitting end to this book. The first lesson is that whatever your position, whether you are in public affairs or not, if you lead people, your job is to manage meaning through framing. You cannot always control what happens in your environment, but you can influence how it is seen. If you do not manage meaning, others will step forward to do so—and they will not always be kind.

Second, the better developed your mental models, the better your framing. Fernald's watchdog groups were better prepared to manage the meaning of the failed implosion because their mental models were better developed for what might transpire. As a result of a contentious history, these activists felt that the government and previous Fernald management firms had failed to deliver on their pledges in the past. Another failed pledge, this time in the form of a failed implosion, was—to their way of thinking—nothing new. Fernald officials, by contrast, never envisioned that the implosion would not be complete and successful.

Third, prepare, anticipate—prime for spontaneity. Failing that, however, if you replay missed opportunities, you can reclaim many leadership moments. Some might argue that after-the-fact framing is not nearly as effective. But just as Fernald's clean-up will not be judged by a single defining event, your leadership will not be judged by a single defining decision. Your leadership will be based upon a series of moments in your everyday work life and the realities you help to construct: image will build upon image, communication upon communication.

Finally, your moral compass will give you the courage of your convictions. Even though the natural reaction to a public embarrassment is to turn inward and clam up, Fernald management was committed to continue forging an open relationship with its stakeholders. They said so publicly because those are the values they have chosen to embrace. It may be a long time before Fernald's relationships with stakeholders are completely repaired, but the company is taking steps in the right direction.

In the same way that Fernald's framing efforts have not always been smooth sailing, you too will encounter rough seas along the way. The convictions you hold, based upon who you are, what you stand for, and your vision for the future, will be like lighthouse beacons viewed from sometimes distant points on the open sea. They will serve as your internal points of reference that will help you communicate in today's turbulent environments. They will be the source of your most effective framing.

References

Alexander, H. G. *Meaning and Language*. Glenview, Ill.: Scott, Foresman, 1969.

Bargh, J. A. "Conditional Automaticity: Varieties of Automatic Influence in Social Perception and Cognition." In J. A. Bargh and J. S. Uleman (eds.), *Unintended Thought*. New York: Guilford Press, 1989.

Bartlett, C. A., and Ghoshal, S. "Changing the Role of Top Management: Beyond Strategy to Purpose." *Harvard Business Review*, Nov./Dec. 1994, pp. 79–88.

Basden, M. D. *Communicative Differences in Participative and Authoritative Leadership*. Unpublished manuscript, University of Cincinnati, 1991.

Bennis, W. *An Invented Life*. Reading, Mass.: Addison-Wesley, 1993.

Bennis, W., and Nanus, B. *Leaders: The Strategies for Taking Charge*. New York; Harper and Row, 1985.

Berg, I. K., and de Shazer, S. "Making Numbers Talk: Language in Therapy." In S. Friedman (ed.), *The New Language of Change*. New York: Guilford Press, 1993.

Bowles, J., and Hammond, J. *Beyond Quality: How 50 Winning Companies Use Continuous Improvement*. New York: Putnam, 1991.

Bricking, T. "Day 2: It's Still Standing." *The Cincinnati Enquirer*, Sept. 12, 1994.

Brydon, S. R. "Spinners on Patrol: Network Coverage in the Aftermath of Presidential and Vice Presidential Debates." Paper presented to the Speech Communication Association conference, San Francisco, Nov. 20, 1989.

Burke, K. "Fact, Inference, and Proof in the Analysis of Literary Symbolism." In L. Bryson (ed.), *Symbols and Values: An Initial Study* (Thirteenth Symposium of the Conference on Science, Philosophy and Religion). New York: Harper and Brothers, 1954.

Burke, K. *The Philosophy of Literary Form*. New York: Vintage Books, 1957.

Burke, K. *A Rhetoric of Motives*. Berkeley: University of California Press, 1962.

Case, R. O., Jr. *Not in My Backyard: The Rhetorical Situation of a Hazardous Waste Incinerator.* Unpublished manuscript, University of Cincinnati, 1993.

Chen, C. C., and Meindl, J. R. "The Construction of Leadership Images in the Popular Press: The Case of Donald Burr and People Express." *Administrative Science Quarterly,* 1991, *36,* 521–551.

Clancy, J. J. *The Invisible Powers: The Language of Business.* Lexington, Mass.: Lexington Books, 1989.

de Shazer, S. *Clues: Investing Solutions in Brief Therapy.* New York: W.W. Norton, 1988.

de Shazer, S. *Putting Difference to Work.* New York: W.W. Norton, 1991.

Deetz, S. "Critical-Cultural Research: New Sensibilities and Old Realities." *Journal of Management,* 1985, *11,* 121–136.

Dickson, P. *War Slang: American Fighting Words and Phrases from the Civil War to the Gulf War.* New York: Pocket Books, 1994.

Dowd, M. "Is 'Slick Willie' Image Now 'Willie the Wimp'?" *The New York Times,* June 4, 1993.

Duck, J. D. "Managing Change: The Art of Balancing." *Harvard Business Review,* Nov./Dec. 1993, pp. 109–118.

Durrant, M., and Kowalski, K. M. "Enhancing Views of Competence." In S. Friedman (ed.), *The New Language of Change.* New York: W.W. Norton, 1993.

Dyer, D. "A Voice of Experience: An Interview with TRW's Frederick C. Crawford." *Harvard Business Review,* Nov./Dec. 1991, pp. 115–126.

Eisenberg, E. "Ambiguity as a Strategy in Organizational Communication." *Communication Monographs,* 1984, *51,* 227–242.

Entman, R. M. "Framing: Toward Clarification of a Paradigm." *Journal of Communication,* 1993, *43,* 51–58.

Erickson, B., Lind, E. A., Johnson, B. C., and O'Barr, W. M. "Speech Style and Impression Formation in a Court Setting: The Effects of 'Powerful' and 'Powerless' Speech." *Journal of Experimental Social Psychology,* 1978, *14,* 266–279.

Fairhurst, G. T. "Echoes of the Vision: When the Rest of the Organization Talks Total Quality." *Management Communication Quarterly,* 1993, *6,* 331–371.

Fairhurst, G. T., Green, S. G., and Snavely, B. K. "Managerial Control and Discipline: Whips and Chains." In M. McLaughlin (ed)., *Communication Yearbook VIII.* Newbury Park, Calif.: Sage, 1984.

Fairhurst, G. T., and Wendt, R. G. "The Gap in Total Quality." *Management Communication Quarterly,* 1993, *6,* 441–451.

Feiertag, J. "Going, Going . . . Still Standing." *Hamilton Journal News,* Sept. 11, 1994.

Fiske, S. T., and Taylor, S. E. *Social Cognition.* New York: McGraw-Hill, 1991.

Gamson, W. A., and Lasch, K. E. "The Political Culture of Social Welfare Policy." In S. E. Spiro and E. Yuchtman-Yaar (eds.), *Evaluating the Welfare State.* San Diego, Calif.: Academic Press, 1983.

Goffman, E. "On Facework: An Analysis of Ritual Elements in Social Interaction." *Psychiatry: Journal for the Study of Interpersonal Processes,* 1955, *18,* 213–231.

Great Photographers. Alexandria, Va.: Time-Life Books, 1971.

Gronn, P. C. "Talk as the Work: The Accomplishment of School Administration." *Administrative Science Quarterly,* 1983, *28,* 1–21.

Hellman, P. "Her Push for Prevention Keeps Kids out of ER," *Sunday Examiner & Chronicle Parade Magazine,* Apr. 18, 1995, pp. 8–10.

Hinterhuber, H. H., and Popp, W. "Are You a Strategist or Just a Manager?" *Harvard Business Review,* Jan./Feb. 1992, pp. 105–113.

Hitt, M. A., Keats, B. W., Harback, H. F., and Nixon, R. D. "Rightsizing: Building and Maintaining Strategic Leadership and Long-Term Competitiveness." *Organizational Dynamics,* 1994, *23,* 18–32.

Hosking, D. M., and Morley, I. E. "The Skills of Leadership." In J. G. Hunt, B. R. Baglia, H. P. Dachler, and C. A. Schrieshiem (eds.), *Emerging Leadership Vistas.* Lexington, Mass.: Lexington Books, 1988.

Iacocca, L., and Novak, W. *Iacocca: An Autobiography.* New York: Bantam Books, 1984.

Jaques, E. "In Praise of Hierarchy." *Harvard Business Review,* Jan./Feb. 1990, pp. 127–133.

Kanter, R. M. *Men and Women of the Corporation.* New York: Basic Books, 1977.

Kanter, R. M. "Championing Change: An Interview with Bell Atlantic's CEO Raymond Smith," *Harvard Business Review,* Jan./Feb. 1991, 119–130.

Kellerman, K. "Communication: Inherently Strategic and Primarily Automatic." *Communication Monographs,* 1992, *59,* 288–300.

Kelly, G. *The Psychology of Personal Constructs,* Vol. 1: *A Theory of Personality.* New York: W.W. Norton, 1955.

Kerwin, K. "The 'Single-Minded Kid' Who's Remaking Ford. *Business Week,* Apr. 3, 1995, p. 101.

Kinsley, M. "Let Them Eat Laptops." *New Yorker,* Jan. 23, 1995, pp. 6–7.

Klein, J. "Walking Small." *Newsweek,* Aug. 3, 1992, p. 29.

Kolodner, J. L., and Riesbeck, C. K. *Experience, Memory and Reasoning.* Hillsdale, N.J.: Erlbaum, 1986.

Kotter, J. "Leading Change: Why Transformation Efforts Fail." *Harvard Business Review,* Mar./Apr. 1995, pp. 59–67.

Kouzes, J. M., and Posner, B. Z. *Credibility: How Leaders Can Gain and Lose It, Why People Demand It.* San Francisco: Jossey-Bass, 1993.

Labich, K. "Will United Fly?" *Fortune,* Aug. 22, 1994, pp. 70–77.

Laborde, G. Z. *Fine Tune Your Brain.* Palo Alto, Calif.: Syntony, 1988.

Lakoff, G., and Johnson, M. *Metaphors We Live By.* Chicago: University of Chicago Press, 1980.

Lee, W. G. "A Conversation with Herb Kelleher." *Organizational Dynamics,* 1994, *23,* 64–74.

Leibovich, M. "You Work, Therefore You Complain." *The Cincinnati Enquirer,* Feb. 3, 1995, p. D3.

Levin, D. "The Real Iacocca." *Newsweek,* May 1, 1995, pp. 62–63.

Lewicki, P., and Hill, T. "Unconscious Processes as Explanations of Behavior in Cognitive, Personality, and Social Psychology." *Personality and Social Psychology Bulletin,* 1987, *13,* 355–362.

Mager, R. F. *Goal Analysis.* Belmont, Calif.: Fearon, 1972.

Martin, J., and Siehl, C. "Organizational Culture and Counterculture: An Uneasy Symbiosis." *Organizational Dynamics,* 1983, *3,* 52–64.

Modic, S. "Cincom Bets Big on People Power: How Tom Nies Defines His CEO Title." *Industry Week,* Aug. 21, 1989, pp. 23–26.

Morgan, G. *Images of Organization.* Newbury Park, Calif.: Sage, 1986.

Nichols, N. A. "Medicine, Management, and Mergers: An Interview with Merck's P. Roy Vagelos." *Harvard Business Review,* Nov./Dec. 1994, pp. 105–114.

Nishiyama, K. "Japanese Quality Circles." Paper presented at the International Communication Association conference, Minneapolis, Minn., May 1981.

O'Keefe, D. J. *Persuasion: Theory and Practice.* Newbury Park, Calif.: Sage, 1990.

Orwell, G. *Shooting an Elephant and Other Essays.* Orlando, Fla.: Harcourt Brace Jovanovich, 1950.

Pascale, R. T., and Athos, A. G. *The Art of Japanese Management.* New York: Warner, 1981.

Pondy, L. R. "Leadership Is a Language Game." In M. W. McCall, Jr., and M. M. Lombardo (eds.), *Leadership: Where Else Can We Go?* Durham, N.C.: Duke University Press, 1978.

Reber, A. S., Allen, R., and Regan, S. "Syntactical Learning and Judgment, Still Unconscious and Still Abstract: Comment on Dulany, Carlson, and Dewey." *Journal of Experimental Psychology: General* 1985, *114,* 17–34.

Riesbeck, C. K., and Schank, R. C. *Inside Case-Based Reasoning.* Hillsdale, N.J.: Erlbaum, 1989.

Safire, W. *The New York Times,* July 21, 1988.

Schank, R. C. *Explanation Patterns: Understanding Mechanically and Creatively.* Hillsdale, N.J.: Erlbaum, 1986.

Schein, E. *Organizational Culture and Leadership: A Dynamic View.* San Francisco: Jossey-Bass, 1985.

Senge, P. M. *The Fifth Discipline.* New York: Doubleday, 1990.

Stains, L. R. "Martina's Final Volley." *USA Weekend,* Aug. 26–28, 1994, pp. 4–6.

Stayer, R. "How I Learned to Let My Workers Lead." *Harvard Business Review,* Nov./Dec. 1990, pp. 66–83.

Stewart, T. A. "Reengineering: The Hot New Managing Tool." *Fortune,* Aug. 23, 1993, pp. 41–48.

Thomas, O. *Metaphor and Related Subjects.* New York: Random House, 1969.

Tompkins, P. K., and Cheney, G. "Communication and Unobtrusive Control in Contemporary Organizations." In R. D. McPhee and P. K. Tompkins (eds.), *Organizational Communication: Traditional Themes and New Directions.* Newbury Park: Sage, 1985.

Walton, M. *The Deming Management Method.* New York: Perigee, 1986.

Walton, S., and Huey, J. *Sam Walton: Made in America.* New York: Doubleday, 1992.

Watzlawick, P., Beavin, J. H., and Jackson, D. D. *The Pragmatics of Human Communication.* New York: W.W. Norton, 1967.

Weick, K. E. *The Social Psychology of Organizing* (2nd ed.). Reading, Mass.: Addison-Wesley, 1979.

Wilkins, A. L. "Organizational Stories as Symbols Which Control the Organization." In P. Frost and others (eds.), *Organizational Culture.* Newbury Park, Calif.: Sage, 1983.

Wilson, S. R., and Putnam, L. L. "Interaction Goals in Negotiation." In J. A. Anderson (ed.), *Communication Yearbook 13.* Newbury Park, Calif.: Sage, 1990.

White, E. M. (ed.). *The Writer's Control of Tone.* New York: W.W. Norton, 1970. (Originally published 1950 by Harcourt, Brace & World)

Wolff, C. "Going, Going . . . Still There!" *The Cincinnati Enquirer,* Sept. 11, 1994.

Wright, J. P. *On a Clear Day You Can See General Motors.* Grosse Point, Mich.: Wright Enterprises, 1979.

Zaleznik, A. "Managers and Leaders: Are they Different?" *Harvard Business Review,* May/June 1977, pp. 126–135.

Index